HOW TO BE A RIGHT BASTARD

Nick Bateman
with Mickey Hutton

Published by John Blake Publishing Ltd,
3 Bramber Court, 2 Bramber Road,
London W14 9PB, England

First published in 2000

ISBN 1903402 263

British Library Cataloguing-in-Publication Data:

A catalogue record for this book is
available from the British Library.

Typeset by t2

Printed in Great Britain by
Creative Print and Design (Wales),
Ebbw Vale, Gwent.

1 3 5 7 9 10 8 6 4 2

Papers used by John Blake Publishing Limited are natural, recy-
clable products made from wood grown in sustainable forests. The
manufacturing processes conform to the environmental regulations
of the country of origin.

With thanks to: Prudence O'Brien.
Gary, Neil, Mark and the Adonis
from Fortified Security.
My family and true friends.

contents

Part One

Nasty Nick and
Big Brother

My name's Nick Bateman. I'm a Scorpio, my favourite colour is green and my hobbies are ... Oh, bollocks to that! The reason you've bought this book is to find out all the dirt on *Big Brother* and to learn how you, too, can be a complete and utter bastard.

Well, before I tell you about the heroes and villains on the hit Channel Four series, let me give you a few secrets as to how I got picked out of 45,000 applicants. Who knows, it may even help you in your quest for stardom and you might make it, too. Well, as long as you don't get in my way.

But, before we start, my full name is Jack Nicholas Guy Bateman. I'm a Scorpio, I'm single, and I was born on 5th November 1967 in Kent. I'm 6ft tall and have green eyes. I have a tattoo of a scorpion on my right shoulder. I was educated at Gordounston and I support Fulham FC. I have six sisters and two brothers, my mother now lives in Hampshire and my father died when I was 21. I still miss him.

It all started when I logged on to the Channel Four website from the offices of the company I worked for in the City. Now, the reason I was connecting to the Internet instead of endeavouring to make my company more money is because I was so bored working there. You see, I was a Lloyd's insurance broker – no, don't nod off, it does get better –

this job was becoming so tedious that I was thinking of packing it all in and going off on a trip to Australia. I think some of my ancestors might have headed the same way. Couple that with the fact I detested my boss (don't we all?), so instead of thinking up ingenious ways of killing him, I decided I'd have a trawl around cyber space. And it was there I saw that Channel Four were looking for outgoing contestants to take part in a new live game show. Well, I had nothing to lose but my City suit, so I sent off the application form.

I got an e-mail back almost instantly asking me if I could send them a two-minute video of myself.

After borrowing a video camera from some friends, (I had to convince them I wasn't making a porn movie so they would lend it to me, but I couldn't tell them about *Big Brother* – I'm still not sure they believed me), I planned how I could make the best impact with my two minutes. I knew I would have to include everything I was interested in and I didn't want to make a fool of myself by telling them lies only to be tripped up later on. So, of course, the only thing to do was a strip. I started with a gag, telling them that I was Nick and I was an alcoholic (OK, it's nearly a gag). Then, as I was explaining about my job in the City, I stripped off my suit off to reveal the white coat I wore when I did my Reiki healing; this I stripped off to reveal my kung fu outfit (I'm very keen on martial arts), and then I stripped down to nothing but a pair of swimming trunks and put on a pair of goggles to let them know that swimming was also one of my hobbies. I mean, how did they think I got this great body? Well I thought my video was a work of genius, how could they resist me? I thought I might even enter it at Cannes; well, you never know, it could win the Palme d'Oorstop award.

I sent the video off and do you know what happened? Absolutely nothing. I thought I had failed miserably so I started sorting out a flight to Oz. Not only that, but my company had sent me on a training course to Teddington Lock. I'd try and explain how tedious this was but you would have to go and lie down in a darkened room. But just as the course was at its most boring, I got a call from *Big Brother* asking me if I could attend an interview at the end of the week. Could I? Nothing would stop me.

The interviews were at a place called The Chloroform Building in the centre of London and I got there early to focus myself (see – scheming even then). And what a motley bunch were there! Some of the contestants were being very loud and there was a lot of staring and posturing going on. I kept myself to myself and tried to remain calm. (I hope you lot are learning something from this.)

We were all called down to the basement level and put into three groups of 24 and played our first game. Names of famous people were attached to our foreheads and by asking 'yes' and 'no' questions we had to guess who they were. I quickly guessed my character's name and won. It'll come as no surprise to you that the name I had to guess was Superman. But, hey, I had been noticed. The next game involved moving an egg from one cup to another with the aid of only a toothpick, an elastic band and a straw. Now, this may sound impossible but remember my team had – well – me and we completed this task so fast that they made us do it again as they thought we had cheated. So we did it again. Faster. Ha! I was really being noticed now. It was just at that moment, when I needed all of my concentration, that I fell head-over-heels, jaw-droppingly, tongue-hanging-out in love. Great timing, Nicholas.

Her name was Rachel and she was another contestant. It really was one of those 'eyes across a crowded room' moments and this was a very crowded room. But we had been told that we couldn't mix with any other candidates so me slinking across to the girl of my dreams and begging her for a date was out of the question. But I had plans.

The next game involved making up a game and our team was asked to elect a captain. Guess who they elected? Me. I felt like shouting across the room, 'Look, Rachel I'm Captain! I'd be a really good husband and a stupendous dad!'. I was already designing our living room. (A cream motif if you must know.) Anyway, my team created fantastic game called Blow Relay Croquet. And I can honestly say that it was not only the best game in the room, but also the best game invented ever and expect to see it on the shelves in time for Christmas.

The next step was another interview in which we were given a huge form and told to take it home, fill it out and send it back to *Big Brother*. Great. I thought they should've picked me there and then after my performance with the team. As I was leaving the building, I noticed that the new 'love of my life' and 'future wife' Rachel was just up ahead of me. I sprinted after her, she turned down a corridor and when I got there she was gone and I never saw her again. (If you're reading this, Rachel, get in touch – I need to know what colour you want the nursery.)

Guess what happened next? Yup, I changed my name to Maureen and went to work as a transvestite lion tamer in Amsterdam.

Oh, don't be daft!

What happened was absolutely nothing. Zero. Zilch. I knew there were a lot of us up for *Big Brother*, but surely Channel Four could process our forms quicker? Didn't they have up-to-the-minute computers or at least really fast work experience kids? This is a good lesson to learn for anyone who wants to get involved in television – there will be a lot of waiting around for other people to make decisions and this will be frustrating.

Back in the real world my work began to deteriorate. I couldn't stand being in my job for much longer and I planned to resign. I still had the idea of going to Australia, but I had a nagging feeling that I was going to end up on *Big Brother*. Anyway I took the plunge and told my boss just where he could put his job. I thought I should try and get some reaction from *Big Brother*, so I called them up and told them what I had done. Guess what happened?

Absolut ... Oh, you know.

Nothing happened.

I was lying on my bed in my flat trying to learn the words to 'Waltzing Matilda', when *Big Brother* finally called. They wanted me to have a meeting with a psychotherapist the very next day.

Great! They'd kept me hanging around for weeks and then wanted me immediately. And I also had to attend a black-tie party that night so I was going to be in a great state for my meeting. But I started to hatch a plan. I attended the party as I had planned and had far too much to drink. This was also part of my plan, but then it usually is. The next morning, when I turned up for the meeting, I arrived dishevelled, still wearing my DJ, on the pretext that I had just flown in from Edinburgh where I had been attending a stag party. As you can imagine, the *Big Brother* team loved this. I was obviously 'so committed to the programme'.

The meeting with the therapist was a breeze. He asked me questions like when did I last cry (I didn't tell him it was through frustration waiting for *Big Brother* to call) and I fenced all the hard questions as best I could, and even asked a few questions of my own, which threw him a bit. He had a very annoying habit of saying 'Hmmm' all the time which we all mimicked when we got into the house. Maybe he should see someone about it. I left the meeting feeling pretty pleased with myself. I knew I had done well.

Then ... nothing happened.

'Waltzing Matilda, waltzing Matilda, you'll come a ...' Ring! Ring!

'Hello? You want me when? Tomorrow. I'll be there.'

Yeah. Lots of hurry up and wait and then I was eventually asked to meet the executive producers of the show. I was kept waiting for an hour (no change there, then) and when I was finally allowed into their presence. They stressed that the people they picked for the show would have to do exactly as they were told. They were very careful to highlight the pros of the show but quickly brushed over the negative effect it could have. I was concerned I hadn't done well enough. But at least things were moving on.

A really strange thing happened next. I wasn't kept waiting. *Big Brother* phoned the next day and asked me if I could do some filming with them. I put the phone down very quietly ... then ran around the room screaming.

Before the filming day, *Big Brother* decided to take me out to lunch. I thought this would be a pleas-

ant way to spend an afternoon but I warned myself
never to let my guard down – which turned out to be
a very good lesson because there were three of us at
lunch that afternoon. And the two producers from
Big Brother played it in a good cop, bad cop style.
They kept telling me I was in the final twenty but
they hadn't decided who had made it through. I felt I
was being really grilled. So, in keeping with the game
plan I was now formulating, I only let them know
what I wanted them to know. If they were going to
play it good cop, bad cop, then I was going to play it
bad Nick, bad Nick. Even though I played it cool, that
day did have an effect on me because I started smok-
ing and drinking again after having given it up for
seven months.

On the day of the filming, I was a nervous wreck.
I had hardly slept the night before but, of course, I
wasn't going to let on to *Big Brother* that I felt like
this. As far as they were concerned, I was quietly confident. I had planned my filming day carefully to
make me look as good as possible. Our first stop was
the kung fu school where I train. Now, I'm no master
of the sport, but I know enough about it to make
myself look good. Especially if the people watching
don't do it at all. I think *Big Brother* were impressed

at my martial arts skills. I certainly pulled the black belt over their eyes!

I knew that after we had been to the kung fu school we were going back to my house to film, so I had cunningly left certain items of interest scattered around the place arranged in such a way to catch *Big Brother*'s eye and make me seem even more fascinating than I am. With the filming at my house over, we then raced to the City and did a few quick filmed inserts, then on to my beloved Fulham FC where I was filmed on their hallowed turf. That was the best bit of the whole experience for me.

Big Brother also wanted to film a select group of my friends talking about me to camera. So it was back to my place where I had gathered my motley bunch of mates to blow my trumpet. And they couldn't have performed any better. They sounded like a brass band. *Big Brother* must've thought I was a cross between Mother Teresa and Bruce Lee.

Once the filming was over, I was absolutely drained, both physically and mentally. But the *Big Brother* crew took my friends and me for a drink to thank us for all our hard work. They seemed quite pleased at how the day had gone and were enthusing all evening. I should've been pleased with myself but

I was so tired all I really wanted to do was crawl into bed and sleep. Which is not like me at all; I'm usually the last one to leave any party!

In the middle of all the celebrations one of the crew pulled me aside and asked if I'd like to know how I'd done. I sleepily thought she was going to tell me how well I'd done that day. But when she whispered that I was in, I didn't really understand what she was talking about. So she had to tell me again, but not too loudly as she wasn't supposed to be doing this at all. I was in! I was in the house! I couldn't believe it and I was immediately wide awake. I wanted to shout it out and tell everyone in the pub but, of course, I couldn't. It even crossed my mind that this might be another test, so I kept quiet. I was in! I was in!

The next day I should have felt fantastic, but I felt awful. After all the excitement of the day before, I was having a real come down. I knew I should be joyously skipping around the flat – after all, I had got what I wanted. But I couldn't shake off my miserable mood. I don't suppose all the alcohol I drank the night before helped either. One of the worst things about the whole thing was that I couldn't tell anyone I was going into the house. If I did and *Big Brother* found out I'd be immediately disqualified and they had plenty of other competitors to take my place. That day was awful, the worst I've ever experienced. I didn't want to talk to anyone but I wanted to tell everyone as well. I just didn't know what to do with myself and finishing off 'Waltzing Matilda' wasn't an option. That night I didn't sleep at all and stayed up listening to music. At dawn, I took a taxi to Wimbledon and watched the sun come up. Now, I don't want to get all mystic on you, but that certainly seemed to help me and I felt a lot calmer. I recommend that everyone does it at least once in their lives.

There was one other little cloud on the horizon. I hadn't told my mum that I had packed in my sensible job in the City and was going to live with nine complete strangers in a house while being watched 24 hours a day by the entire nation. Imagine what your mum would say? Exactly. I was terrified. I reckon if Hitler had told his mum that he was going to invade Poland, she would've smacked the back of his legs and sent him packing. Anyway, when I finally plucked up courage to tell her she wasn't pleased at all. She thought it was a very bad idea and told me in no uncertain terms. She slammed the phone down and wouldn't speak to me at all. Sorry, Mum but it's my life. I'm not a five-year-old.

With a week left to go before entering the house, I couldn't relax at all. But there was one thing I could do and that was work out my game plan and how I was going to get everyone else thrown out of the house. I was sure they would be doing exactly the same thing.

Then all the waiting around really started getting to me. I was dying to get into the house. All I did was hang around the house watching TV. The show 15 to 1 seemed to be on all the time. I now can't bear to see William G Stewart. He drives me mad. Life took on a surreal edge; it was as though I was living in a bubble. No one else's life seemed to matter. My mobile never stopped ringing. *Big Brother* was always enquiring after my well-being and friends were calling up wishing me luck. I had been packed for days.

Some of my friends took me out for a meal. They were calling it 'The Last Supper'. But I couldn't concentrate or join in. When they started to guess how long I would last in the house, I got a bit upset when some of them suggested that I wouldn't last a week. As you can see, I was a right bundle of laughs to be around.

The day before we went into the house, I thought

I was going mad but I knew I had to keep cool and see this thing through. I had packed and re-packed and had my game plan worked out. I was ready. I was collected by taxi and taken to a hotel for a final briefing. I was given my radio mike and had loads of photographs taken of me in various poses. They even took photos of my hands and feet. I hoped this was so some 'expert' could determine my character through the prints and not so I could be identified later on when someone in the house went mad and chopped us all up.

At the briefing, I was informed I would be paid £30 a day for appearing on the show. That's £1.25 per hour! It's well below the minimum wage. That didn't bother me, as I was going to win!

I was taken by my chaperone to the Blind Beggar pub in the East End of London. This, of course, is the pub made famous by the slaying of George Cornell by the Krays in the Sixties. I was surprised at how small the pub really was because if you talk to anyone from the East End, they all claim to have been there on that fateful night, so in actual fact the pub should be able to hold thousands of people!

I was really pleased that some friends of mine had turned up to see me off. We had a few drinks until my chaperone insisted that I go back to the hotel as I was on a 10.00pm curfew. When we got back, I said 'Goodnight' to him and went to my room. For five minutes. Then I sneaked back to the hotel bar for another two hours' drinking. I couldn't let my last night of freedom pass soberly ...

Well, it was here at last. The day when I finally entered the house and got to meet my fellow house-mates and adversaries. I was collected in car number eight and driven to the glamorous location of Tesco's car park where I was met by nine other similar cars. We were besieged by the press and photographers but slowly the cortège moved into the studio. We arrived, climbed out of the cars, and I promptly dropped my radio mike. (How cool is that?) The whole area was lit up by the photographer's flashguns. Our friends and family were there, shouting out our names – except my mum, of course. The reporters were all trying to get us to give some sort of quote – it was complete bedlam. Our bodyguards pulled us towards the house. We entered and, without warning, the door slammed behind us. That was it – we were in.

It's hard to express all the emotions that were going through my mind at that precise moment. My first reaction was to try to make friends but I knew that, at some stage, I would be trying to oust them, so I decided to hang back a bit and watch their reactions to their surroundings. I was also desperate to go to the loo, but the thought of having to go while being watched by a camera really put me off. It took me three attempts. But I had to go and, in the end, I was the first to go which made it a bit easier for the others.

Talking about going to the loo, later on in the house, someone kept pissing in the shower. It drove everyone mad. Well, that was me. Sorry, guys!

At first, we all ran around the place exploring our surroundings and, I suppose, sussing each other out at the same time. I immediately got a feel of who my allies in the house would be, so I subtly started trying to get as much information about them all while they were still new and at their most vulnerable. Little did I know that other people also had the same plan.

The first thing we did as a team was to sort out who was sleeping where. Craig and Andy were cracking obvious jokes about going in with the girls. We all decided that the boys should have the room with the double bed as it would be more comfortable for Darren, as he was the biggest of the household. We were being nice and polite to each other at this stage.

That was soon to change. I went into the bedroom to make up my bed and I found that I had no bottom sheet. So I nicked Andy's. When Andy found he had no bottom sheet, he nicked Craig's. Sneaky, eh? Poor old Craig never realised what we'd done and I knew I'd have to keep an eye on Andy.

The first night in the house was like being back at boarding school but without the beatings and the buggery. Even with Darren rabbiting on like a big girl, Andy talking about which of the girls he'd like to shag and Craig letting go some of the loudest farts I'd ever heard in my life, I had the best night's sleep I'd had in months now that all the waiting was over. I'd set my alarm clock to go off really early so I would be the first in the showers, as they were only on for an hour a day. I wanted to be up early anyway, because you know what they say – the early bird gets every-one kicked out of the house.

Our first day and *Big Brother* set us our first task. We had to make a mug and a bowl. Us blokes got straight down to it, while the girls ... er ... sunbathed. I don't think that they had grasped this task thing and it was because of their laziness that we failed. Well, that and the fact that the pottery blew up in the oven. I was furious but put on a brave face especially for the camera.

We had also seriously underestimated how much food ten people would consume. We thought it would be sensible to spend 60% of our allowance on booze and 40% on food. I still think this is a sensible idea. I wanted to buy nice bottles of wine but Nichola and Caroline, with their refined tastes, wanted to buy cheap cider and lots of it. I don't think they'll be offered a stint presenting *Food and Drink*, unless they have a new section called 'How To Get Pissed and Lairy Quickly'.

Of course, the lack of food and too much to drink was starting to cause tension in the house, especially with Sada reminding us every ten minutes that she had a boyfriend and that she was writing a book and how bloody wonderful tofu was. And *Big Brother* kept reminding Sada to wear her radio mike. Bloody hippies! It was no use, she'd have to go.

The bright lights in the house were playing havoc with our body clocks and we started going to bed later and later. Tiredness was making us very irritable. The first big fight kicked off when Darren nicked some of Sada's beans and she started screaming at him. And she had a boyfriend and she was writi ... Shut up!

By now, everyone's little faults and habits were starting to show: Caroline with that dreadful laugh; Mel with her flirting; Andy with his incessant talk about sex; Craig, well, for just being dim; Darren and his ingratiating way; Anna with her holier-than-thou attitude (Well, she was an ex-nun so I suppose that was to be expected); Nichola who was just loud; Sada ... oh, you know; and Tom. Well, we never saw Tom. He never spoke, cooked or did anything. I was really keeping an eye on him. Surely he must have a fantastic plan to get us all out of the house.

The day of the first nomination was drawing near and we were passing the time by playing a card game called Cheat which I excelled at. Funny that. I had managed to draw Tom out of his shell a bit by getting him to play cards and it didn't go unnoticed that he was an excellent player.

Our next task was a memory test. Each house member had to give us some information about themselves, such as what was their favourite film or their pet hate. We had to memorise them all. Each of us took it in turns to go into the diary room and *Big Brother* asked us three random questions from the list. We all had to get it 100% right. Craig failed us. He got one wrong. We knew he would be really embarrassed if he thought he had let us down, so we didn't tell him his score. *Big Brother*, wanting to get some sort of reaction, let him know immediately. Craig was gutted.

I realised then that *Big Brother* would use any situation to try to elicit some reaction on screen and also how important the tasks could be, as anyone who wasn't pulling their weight in the house would be a target for eviction, especially when there was food and booze involved. The day of the nominations were really tense and when Sada and Caroline's names were announced by *Big Brother*, it kicked off big time.

Nichola went ballistic because, by now, she and Caroline had formed a friendship and she demanded to know who had voted for her new best mate. Sada and Caroline took the nominations very badly and there were lots of tears. Under the guise of caring, sharing, Nick I comforted the girls. This was purely tactical as I didn't want the survivor voting me out and I said exactly the same things to them both. The atmosphere in the house was horrendous with no communication between the girls or boys. The girls were particularly annoyed because they were convinced that it would be one of the boys who would be evicted – it was obvious they had clearly discussed their nominations with each other. Sada started to tell anyone who would listen, including the voting public at home, that she wanted to go home. If this was some sort of tactical ploy, it was probably the worst idea since someone said, 'Ooh I know. We'll build a ship so big that icebergs will bounce off it and we'll call it the Titanic.' She was out.

Hooray! That bloody hippie's gone. One down, eight more to go. We were starting to realise that the show was bigger than we thought. By now we could hear the crowd outside the house. They would shout out the names of their favourite house member. At night, people coming back from the pub would shout aggressively.

By day, there was nothing much to do. All we did was drink endless cups of tea, which Caroline always seemed to have on the go. No wonder none of us were sleeping. We read and re-read what magazines we had in the house, although we had to be sure we hid them from Nichola or she would cut them up and use them in one of her ridiculous artistic creations.

I then realised what a difference it made losing even one member of the house, as now everyone seemed so much more relaxed. I began to give Reiki healing because I knew it meant I could be on a one-to-one with my competitors and maybe I could influence them a bit. I also knew it would be a vote winner with the audience at home. You know - me with my healing hands. It makes me virtually a saint. But, more importantly, it was the only time we were allowed to take our microphones off so no one could hear what we were saying. Hee hee hee! Well, just as everything was ticking along nicely, wouldn't you know, it's nomination time again.

And the nominations are: Andy and Caroline. Fan-fucking-tastic. I'd done it again. The house was in uproar, Caroline went into decline and we were all at each other's throats.

I had a gut feeling that Andy would be getting kicked out of the house next. All his talk of sex was too much even for me. Every time he opened his mouth I could see the girls stiffen, especially Anna who, by now, had told us all that not only was she an ex-nun, but a lesbian. The Lord certainly does move in mysterious ways, eh? And what a waste of a good-looking woman.

Craig in his 'hilarious' way told Anna that all she really needed was a good shagging to cure her. That went down as well ... well ... as well as a lesbian, I suppose. But when Andy told us all that he had been wanking in the house, I knew he had sealed his fate. Mel was upset at Andy's nomination because she obviously fancied him and flirted with him at every opportunity. But she started to cool off a bit when she realised her ally could be going on the long walk. I spent more time than I'd have liked consoling Caroline. I even made the ultimate sacrifice by asking her to play me a tune on her sax. For that alone, I deserve to be made a saint.

Just as night follows day and a farty smell follows Craig, Friday rolled round again. My hunch was right – Andy was out. Thank heavens I had been cultivating Caroline.

I thought it a great shame that Andy was going as we had become good friends. Andy couldn't believe he was out. He really thought everyone in the house loved him. His massive ego had taken a severe bashing. Right up until the moment he was walking out of the door with his suitcase packed he thought that it had been a mistake. Everyone had packed some sort of bright outfit to wear when they left. But not Andy. He left looking like a reject from Marks and Spencer's – he was so confident that he was going to win. He really was that big-headed. As he left he didn't look back. To Andy's credit, though, he gave me his secret stash of cigarettes. This surprised me as he was a non-smoker. Cheeky bugger. He probably thought he would use the cigarettes as bribes later on in the game. Ha! Bye bye, Andrew.

It became obvious that the girls voted for the person they most disliked and the boys voted for the person they would least like to sleep with. (Men, shallow? Never!)

The next person I had to get on side was Craig as I thought that because of our backgrounds (him – oiky, thick builder; me – refined Gordounston-educated City boy). I thought that it could drive a wedge between us. Obviously, he would craft the wedge with his gnarled, son-of-the-soil hands, whereas I would order a silver one from Tiffany. (I'm sorry, I couldn't resist it. It's a joke. Lighten up.)

It was quite difficult to pin down Craig because he spent the whole time in bed. I think it was his way of dealing with the pressures of living in the house – or he could have been keeping up with his farting practice. Not that he needed it. I finally got him into conversation about martial arts, something he adored, and I offered to train with him early in the morning. The reasoning behind this was so that I could quiz him about the other house members without us being overheard. Ooh, I'm sneakier than a box of foxes. With all the training together, Craig and I got quite close, but he had no idea of my ulterior motive.

People in the house had formed little cliques and there were a couple of arguments when Tom and I were caught having a couple of sneaky cigarettes we shouldn't have had and the girls were caught eating chocolates and drinking champagne. I bet the fizzy stuff was a shock for Nichola's cider-hardened palate. I noticed the cameras in the house were following me more than anyone else so I knew I was doing something right. I started to play little games with them like standing stock still trying to get *Big Brother* to think the camera had broken down and the picture had frozen. Or asking in a loud whisper if anyone wanted to come and use my phone. Anything to alleviate the boredom. Little did I realise the mass public hysteria and outrage that my little phone joke had caused. And all that scheming really takes it out of you.

I was, of course, blissfully unaware of the tabloid campaign to have me evicted from the house.

Darren got a big boost one day when some children stood outside the house chanting his name. But then, cruelly, in my estimation, *Big Brother* showed us a video of one of his children's birthday parties. Another example of *Big Brother* trying to get a reaction. Darren was really upset. I was really annoyed, as I knew this would boost his standing with the viewers. Oh, and he obviously did have kids. Now there's a thing!

With Andy gone, the house was even quieter when we were given our next task which was learning semaphore. I truly wished Andy was back as I had been partnered with the dreadful Nichola.

When we were supposed to be learning semaphore, Nichola spent the time sticking silly patterns on the wall instead of knuckling down to the job in hand. On the morning of the task, I found out that Caroline and Nichola had been up all night. This behaviour was selfish and irresponsible and I was furious that we failed the task but overjoyed that Nichola and Caroline had made lots of new enemies.

Because of Nichola and Caroline's behaviour, we had even less food than normal and even less of Nichola's beloved cider. Lack of food was the main cause of arguments in the house. We'd fight over whether we should have peanut butter or jam. All of us would try and stockpile little treats for ourselves.

Mel was always hiding the cheese, like the minx she is. But I'd always find it and eat it.

Big Brother had started giving us the most mundane little tasks like making sunscreens out of bits of manky old netting or setting us inane topics of conversation like 'Which are better – cats or dogs?'

It was driving us all mad. With the nominations coming up, I knew I had to shift my plans up a gear. The house dynamic had completely changed – Tom, Mel and I were in one group and Darren, Caroline and Nichola were in another, and Craig was stuck in the middle. I put my plan into action. I wrote down my nominations and showed them to Tom and Mel. Nichola had to go. Interestingly enough, it was Tom who didn't follow my lead to the letter.

Everyone's behaviour was becoming more and more erratic, especially Nichola who I was sure was becoming psychotic. Without warning, she would explode and start screaming at everyone. If any of the boys had shown this level of aggressive behaviour, I have no doubt that they would have been evicted immediately.

Darren became more and more sycophantic towards the girls. He really laid it on thick, always telling them stories about his granny or mum. And he was incredibly narcissistic. Tom had come out of his shell and was becoming much more confident. Craig was, er, still farting. At around this time, Anna played her trump card. She broke down, telling everyone that she wanted to leave the house. What a stroke of genius! The viewers would love her.

Well, now it started to get interesting. If you are thinking of going into television, remember this – it's all about the edit. The events you saw on TV certainly aren't consistent with what really happened in the house.

What you saw was that Tom was in the diary room voicing his concerns. I had told him to do this to help him stay in the house. Show his vulnerable side. I thought it would keep him on my side. The next minute he's in bed telling Craig about the paper I showed him. It was splashed across every newspaper in Britain. They had been proved right. I was the devil.

No matter how sympathetic *Big Brother* said they were to us, the bottom line was that they were making a television show and that was what they cared about most of all. That's OK, I understood that and I have a saying: 'Those who live by the sword, must die by the sword.' I was certain I could hear swords – or should that be daggers – being unsheathed.

I knew there was something wrong when Craig called a house meeting for the next day. I wasn't unduly concerned as Craig had a bit of a reputation for getting upset about the most trivial things. Like the girls nagging him about not cleaning up his porridge bowl; it was like living with the three bears. When I asked him what he wanted to talk about, he just said that he was unhappy. But I knew it was serious because he had stopped farting.

The next day, as we sat around the table chatting about, well, whatever you can chat about when you've been cooped up with people for four weeks, Craig suddenly blurted out, 'I'm very disappointed in you Nick!'

Now, because I, like everyone else in the house, was used to Craig coming out with the most incredible stories, I thought this was just going to be another tall tale and if it concerned me, I was confident that I could easily bluff my way out of any accusations he was going to throw at me. I was pretty confident, because the week before, when all of us had been sitting in the garden sunning ourselves, I had asked them what they thought of me (game plan) and they all said they really liked me and I brought a lot to the house. They even signed the cookery book I had brought in with supportive messages.

But as I looked around the table at everyone's stern faces, I realised it was a lot more serious than I'd thought. The game was up. I was thinking fast.

They all started at once. How could I do it? Why did I do it? What else had I done? Darren was furious that I'd smuggled in a pencil as he had wanted to write a note to his kids but had no means of doing so. I just sat and took it all. Didn't they realise this was a game show? After they'd all said their piece, I stood up and told them I was leaving the house. I left the table and headed towards the boys' bedroom to a stunned silence. (Remember, I'm still playing the game. I'd have loved to have seen the faces of *Big Brother*.)

After I'd finished packing, I thought I'd better go out and defend myself. (Still playing.) I made an impassioned speech to my housemates. I told them that, because I was the youngest of a very competitive family (surely having six sisters and two brothers should count for something) and the fact that I had worked in a job that demanded the best, I should get another chance. (Possibly some of the best acting ever witnessed?) But, by the looks on their faces they weren't to be swayed. It was then I knew I had to appeal to *Big Brother*.

I went into the diary room and offered them a compromise, and it was this: I would leave the house the following Friday and go through the Davina, friends and family thing every other person who had been evicted had gone through. They said they would get back to me. This was obviously not in their game plan.

Meanwhile, Craig and Nichola were telling the cameras in the house that if either of them were evicted, they would both go. The Internet site was shut down. *Big Brother* had a big problem.

As you can imagine, the atmosphere in the house was awful. *Big Brother* obviously had not expected anything like this to happen. So much for all the so-called experts who had been drafted on to the show. Couldn't they have predicted this was going to happen by reading the photographs of our feet or something? After a three-hour wait (what were they doing? Surely they weren't trying to make us suffer to get good television?) *Big Brother* called me to the diary room and told me I had one hour to pack. I was out.

I was very sad that I was going, but relieved that I

was getting back to the real world. I still felt I'd been betrayed by my housemates for playing the game. Didn't they know why we were there? So, not for me the walk out of the *Big Brother* house and into the arms of adoring fans. No. For me it was sneaking out of the back door and into the arms of Davina McCall. Oh, and for all you fashion victims ... the jeans I was wearing which seemed to have caused so much of a stir and that no-one could identify were by Moschino.

To tell you the truth, I didn't recognise Davina when she came running towards me, arms outstretched I only realised it was her by the tattoo she has on her wrist. She was treating me like a returning war hero.

Davina interviewed me straight away and I was very impressed at her technique; she didn't pull any punches. The first thing she asked me was if I had been a plant. I told her I was a plant for Channel 5 and, for a split-second, she believed me. I was just trying to soften her up. It didn't work and she gave me a real grilling.

The next 24 hours were very uncomfortable. I never realised how much I was hated. I was whisked away to a hidden location and I was a bit perturbed to find I had been assigned two bodyguards. I mean, really! Two bodyguards! All I had done was to try and manipulate a game show. I'm not a murderer.

As the days rolled on, I found myself doing press conference after press conference. (Surely there must have been other things happening in the world?) I realised that I was the most hated man in Britain. And I loved it. Everyone needs a bogeyman and I was it. I could imagine mums telling their kids that, if they weren't good, Nasty Nick would come and get them. That suits me. I'm still using my game plan.

So what do I think about appearing on *Big Brother* now? It was fantastic and I would do it all over again. And I would try to be even more scheming. For anyone out there who is seeking fame and fortune, I would say try to get it any cost but always have a plan. But you must remember: if you are in front of the camera there is a vast army of people who have put you there and it is very hard to survive under the hot flashlights of permanent publicity. It's the people who are behind the camera – the producers, directors, researchers who will go on working long after you are cast on to the 'Guest on *Blankety Blank*' scrapheap.

And to all of my detractors, I would just like you

to remember the words from one the greatest songs ever written and sung by one of one of the greatest singers of all time. I am, of course, referring to the wonderful Joe Dolce and his song 'Shadappa Your Face' ... Oh, it's a joke. Lighten up.

Right, I'm off to make a million.

the players

Andy
(Bart)

As soon as I set eyes on Andy, I knew it was love at first sight. (Obviously, in an 'all blokes together, down the rugby club, punching each other on our manly shoulders, drinking gallons of lager and ogling girls type of way'.) It happened as I was getting out of my car just before we all went into the house for the first time. I dropped my radio mike and it crashed to the floor. As I looked up to see if anyone had seen what I'd done, I saw Andy smiling at me and there was a spark between us. I liked him instantly even though he actually thought I was a member of the production crew and I thought how odd his hair looked with that little patch of grey he has on his fringe. Funnily enough, I have an almost identical patch of grey on the right-hand side of my head. I really noticed it when we were all sitting around the table on the day of the big showdown.

Thinking back, I realise that I liked Andy because he was so much like me. Even though I knew he would be a threat I couldn't help liking him. He always had a half smirk on his face as if he could see something funny that you couldn't. I knew he had hidden depths and that we could have some fun together. The first thing Andy and I did together was polish off the drinks we had brought in with us that afternoon. Then we started to explore the house trying to find places where there weren't any cameras or if there were dead spots where we couldn't be seen. I thought that the whole competition would finally be between Andy and me. Got that slightly wrong, eh? I think that Andy's downfall was purely because of his arrogance and his massive ego. He thought he was unbeatable. But he did bring a great deal to the house, much more than anyone else I thought.

When *Big Brother* set us our first task of making a mug and a bowl each, Andy proved to be really good at it. He even tried to help everyone else with theirs. He was always the first to offer to cook and clean and he even enjoyed gardening. He never stopped. But soon his busy-ness started to annoy certain people in the house. I could tell that Darren and Craig didn't like him from the start. Craig especially because he likes to think of himself as a bit of a joker but Andy was always rushing around and cracking jokes. He kept quoting lines from his favourite TV show *The Simpsons*. And he was proving to be just as annoying as his favourite character Bart.

It was obvious from the word go that Mel really fancied Andy and they were always flirting with each other. But I think she began to cool towards him when he started to get too laddish. He was always the instigator of the practical jokes we played, like putting bowls of water over the doors or taking planks out of each other's beds. The girls weren't too happy when, at the suggestion of Andy all the boys jumped naked into the girl's beds. I'm suprised we all didn't just pole vault back out again!

But I think Andy became his own worst enemy, mainly because he couldn't stop showing off, especially about his sex life and his sexual conquests. He kept going on and on about how had he slept with Filipino prostitutes and how he had taken part in three in a bed sex romps. And then, when he started on about how much he masturbated and how he had even masturbated in the house and didn't care if the cameras saw him or not, I think this was too much for everyone, especially the viewers.

Andy was absolutely stunned when he was nominated. His ego was severely dented. He thought he was absolutely indispensable to the house and when he was actually voted out he couldn't quite take it in. I carefully took in just how Andy had gone wrong and planned to use my new-found knowledge as a weapon against everyone else.

After Andy had gone I really missed him. I missed his competitiveness and his sense of fun – he had been a good adversary. Interestingly enough, after I had been ejected from the house, I met up with Andy in Bagshot for a drink. As usual, I was surrounded by people asking for autographs and photographs and Andy got really annoyed that no-one recognised him. This, of course, was just how I liked it.

Anna
(The Lesbian
Skateboarding Nun)

When I first set eyes on Anna, I really thought she was gorgeous. I had a fantasy that she might even like me. Imagine. We could win the prize money, run off together and live happily ever after in a castle. Fantastic. And my plan would have worked, too, if it hadn't been for those pesky kids. Oh, sorry. I mean if Anna hadn't been a lesbian. Damn you, nature, and your tricks.

Oh, plus the fact that Anna had once been a nun. Cor, talk about putting obstacles in a bloke's way. It did cross my mind when she told us about her God-bothering past that it might be quite difficult getting the better of someone who has the Lord on their side.

Anna was the quietest of all the girls. Mind you, a fully grown gorilla dragging a sackful of coconuts through a herd of sheep in an iron foundry would've been quieter than that lot. She did keep herself to herself but was still very easy to talk to. I think it was because she worked in personnel (in a skateboarding company. Now there's a first; a lesbian, skateboarding nun). It made her a good listener. Everybody else in the house just wanted to hear the sound of their own voices, so Anna was a breath of fresh air. I think what let

Anna down was that she revealed too much too soon, although I don't think she meant to; she just couldn't resist telling everyone that she was gay. And if I'd been a nun I would have certainly held it back as my secret weapon. Mind you, if I had have been a nun, I think I would have flogged my story to the Sunday papers years ago.

I became aware that Anna was just as scheming as me when, as I was secretly observing her one night when she was reading, it suddenly stuck me that she was just pretending to be engrossed in her book. In actual fact, she was listening to everything that was going on around her. I found this very disturbing and thought that I'd better keep an eye on her. I tried on a number of occasions to get a bit closer to Anna to see what made her tick, but this proved impossible. If you tried to get anything at all out of her that she didn't want you to know, she would explode and storm off. Anna could be incredibly pig-headed and competitive.

I first got suspicious about Anna's competitive streak after she revealed she had once been a semi-pro netball player, coupled with the fact that she was a very, very good card player (surely they can't teach you that in nun school). It suddenly dawned on me after watching her at work that she was the female version of me, and I have to take my hat off to her for that. But she was actually more scheming than me, and in a much more underhand way. Anna had the great trick of never being too controversial but always using drama to her best advantage. This was probably most evident when she burst into tears insisting that she wanted to leave the house. Which, of course, meant the rest of her housemates leapt to support her, begging her not to leave and I can imagine the viewers sobbing along with Anna (or Julie Andrews, as I had now come to think of her).

One thing we all liked about Anna was the fact that she could play guitar (ooh, it's just like *The Sound Of Music* isn't it?) and we all liked a singalong, but Anna really knew how to milk it.

Anna showed the real side to her personality after she'd been slagging off Darren and then she was seen giving him a big cuddle. Good tactics, though. I think that as the smell of the money got stronger, so did Anna.

Caroline and Nichola
(The Nutters)

I know I've given everyone else a chapter on their own, but I can never think about Caroline without thinking of Nichola and vice versa. Though, to tell you the truth, I try not to think of either of them too much. It could cause nightmares. Well, look at them!

The first time I saw Caroline and Nichola they were together, of course. They must have just gravitated towards each other. (I wouldn't like to visit the planet with that sort of gravity.) And I thought, Who the fuck are they?

They were the loudest (and I mean that in the way they dressed and in the noise they made) women I had ever met. Caroline with that dreadful (it seemed to me) put-on laugh and Midlands accent (even people from the Midlands have complained to me about how she spoke and hyenas have objected about the laugh); and Nichola with her northern screech and aggressive look.

As soon as Caroline got into the house she put up loads of photos of her family. I did admire her for that little trick, as I thought that it might get some sympathy from the viewers. But surely no-one has that many family members. She also unpacked her saxophone! Now I do like a bit of music and I really like hearing the saxophone played by a good saxophone player. It wasn't as if Caroline couldn't play it. It was just that she could only play one song – 'Killing Me Softly' – and it was killing us all, but not softly. You never knew when Caroline would strike up with her own special version of the song which we all grew to hate. Funnily enough, when I got out of the house, 'Killing Me Softly' came on my car radio and it sent shivers up my spine. I had to turn the radio off as thoughts of Caroline were affecting my driving.

Andy even confided in me that he thought Caroline had smuggled drugs into the house as sometimes her and Nichola's eyes looked a bit strange and they had extreme mood swings, but I assured him that it was just the after effects of the sax playing and all of our eyes looked like that. And we were certainly all starting to go a bit mad because of it.

Caroline didn't just stop at the saxophone as an instrument of torture. She would also sing, which was fine, but she only ever sang the first two lines of any song. Now she said she was a professional singer but she must have had the shortest show of any performer on stage, what with her two-line songs. I suppose she could always pad the show out with 'Killing Me Bloody Softly' on the sax. I always got the impression that Caroline was using the show to kick-start what was left of her fading singing career.

Even though Caroline and Nichola seemed very alike, they did have some completely different traits. For instance, Caroline was a bit of a prude. She would keep her knickers on in the shower and she tried to rig up a curtain in the girls' bedroom so they couldn't see her get undressed. I wonder what she had to hide? Nichola, of course, was the complete opposite and would get her kit off at the drop of a hat and was always wanting to play strip poker.

The first time that things turned really nasty in the house was down to Caroline and Nichola's scheming after the first nominations when Sada and Caroline got nominated. Caroline and Nichola had obviously planned to try and keep each other in the house, so when Caroline's name came up Nichola went absolutely crazy and rampaged around the house demanding to know who had nominated Caroline. The atmosphere in the house became unbearable. And Sada and Caroline were frequently reduced to tears because of the added pressure.

Where Caroline liked to be the centre of attention at all times (she always seemed to speak in
sound bites and was always well framed in a camera), Nichola would frequently go off and do her
own thing, like her papier mâché 'art', and she
seemed to be getting more and more psychotic,
especially towards the men. This got worse with her
PMT, and the lack of sleep, chocolate and alcohol.
We were all very wary of Nichola, 'The Mad One' as
we nicknamed her.

Things came to a head one day after a friendly
pillow fight when Nichola just flipped and started
screaming that we were all wankers with the veins
in her forehead and neck bulging and her eyes staring madly. It occurred to me that there was only one
'wanker' in the house at that moment, and that was
her.

I think everyone in the house breathed a collective sigh of relief when Caroline was finally ousted.
Well, she had been nominated three times. But before
she left and encouraged by her side-kick Nichola, she
demanded to know who had nominated her. We all, of
course, kept schtum. Strangely enough, after
Caroline had gone Nichola's behaviour improved and

while I wouldn't exactly want to sit with her and have a cosy chat, she certainly became less manic. All I had to do now was get rid of her. (Insert your own mad laughter here.)

There was a odd turn of events a few weeks later after all three of us had been evicted from the house. We all met up at the *TV Quick* awards, at which I was guest presenting. I think Caroline and Nichola were a bit miffed that they hadn't been asked to present anything and, as I was doing my announcement, they started drunkenly heckling. Later that evening at the party afterwards, they made complete fools of themselves in front of all the TV bigwigs by careering drunkenly around the dance floor and crashing into the newly skinny Vanessa Feltz, sending her flying. I thought Vanessa was going to punch them. Although since she's lost weight I don't suppose she can hit as hard as she used to. I was very pleased to see some highly unflattering photographs of Nichola and Caroline in all the tabloids the next day.

I think the girls were annoyed that I hadn't risen to them baiting me but, you see, girls, we may have left the house but I'm still using my game plan.

Craig
(The Incredible
Sleeping Man)

If you look in any reference book and find the phrase 'cheeky northerner', there will certainly be a picture of Craig under the heading. Fifty years ago he would have been treading the boards in the music halls as a comic, probably calling himself something like Cuddly Craig, the Cheeky Chappie. I don't think he would have lasted long, though, because Craig thought he was the funniest thing to come out of Liverpool since, well, er, the last funny thing to come out of Liverpool. He told some of the most boring stories I have ever heard in my life and, just to make sure you would remember them, he told them over and over again. I seriously considered going over the wall when Craig started reminiscing.

His favourite story was the one about the time he was on holiday in Cyprus (I don't know if you've ever been to Cyprus, but I'm sure it's a retirement place for old hamburger restaurants – Craig and his refined palate loved it.) Anyway, Craig ended up bonking some girl on a boat. Imagine his surprise when, unbeknown to him and his partner, all the rocking caused the boat to end up on the shore so they were in full view of all the holidaymakers. Oooh, my aching ribs. Oh, and he also reckoned that it took the boat an hour to get to shore. Yeah, righto. More like a couple of minutes. Mind you, I've heard that story soooo often I think I was there.

Now Craig wasn't exactly the brightest member of the household but he more than made up for that with his brawn – when he actually used it. Because, for a while, all Craig ever did was sleep. We used to call him 'the incredible sleeping man'. We hardly ever saw him but we could always hear him because of his incessant farting, which he always tried to do as loudly as he could. I'm sure he could easily win awards for the volume of his wind-breaking. It's a shame there isn't a farting Olympics, because Craig would certainly be a gold medal winner.

As you can imagine, the girls weren't too impressed with Craig's skill. But what they were impressed with was his body and pretty good it was, too, and he never missed a chance to show it off. Women, eh? Not impressed by farting but they like a well-turned pec. No wonder us men will never understand them.

Craig was a really nice bloke with a good heart, which was most clearly shown when he donated his entire prize winnings of £70,000 to a friend with Down's Syndrome, who needed to go to America for a heart and lung transplant. And he did it live on television – perhaps he's not so stupid after all! He never lost his temper, not even when he was being goaded by the terrible twosome Caroline and Nichola; but I think because he was a Scouse builder he had a real chip on his shoulder and found it hard to relate to someone like me with my upbringing. But as far as I was concerned, I wanted him out of the house. We have all since found out the reason that he was in the house in the first place was because if he won, he was going to donate the prize money to a young girl to enable her to go to the Sates to have a heart-lung transplant. But what can you say? He won everyone over with his grand gesture when he won, so I suppose it's a case of (assuming a Cockney accent): 'Gawd bless 'im e's a saint an' no mistake.'

Darren
(The Count)

When I first saw Darren, I couldn't believe how big he was; he looked as if he was two blokes welded together. At 6ft I'm not exactly puny, but Darren towered over me. I also thought he looked really aggressive, even more so than Nichola, and that's going some. The reality is, of course, completely different. As soon as Darren opened his mouth, I knew he was a pussycat and I breathed a sigh of relief. The last thing I wanted was another bloke with a strong personality in the house.

The first thing Darren did after getting through the door was to go to everyone and congratulate them for getting into the house. He was being pathetically nice to everyone and, at first, I had the idea he was quite camp, but when he started to talk about his three kids I thought I had read him wrong. But the weird thing is that he didn't bring any photographs of his kids with him. Now considering we had all brought some momentoes of our families with us, I did think this a bit odd, but then I started to think that maybe this was part of his game plan. Damn, I thought, why didn't I use the kiddy-winky angle? You've got to admit, it's a good one.

I did like Darren's daft, childish sense of

humour, but he could be very two-faced. He loved to play practical jokes but would always blame someone else if he was found out. Sometimes he would instigate the jokes but not carry them out, so someone else got caught.

Darren loved to be the centre of attention and hated it if everyone wasn't focusing on him. His favourite trick was to stand naked in front of the mirror rubbing coconut oil into his body. And I'm here to report that he had nothing to write home about! We had a saying in the house – self-praise is no recommendation – and that certainly applied to Darren as he was always telling us how wonderful he was.

One of the strangest attention-seeking activities I saw Darren engaged in was when he told us all that he had a chicken phobia. Now, a true phobia is a very serious disorder and can cause the sufferer years of trauma. So, because we had chickens in the garden we all felt really sorry for him. But within hours of him telling us of his fear, he had one on his shoulder like a pantomime parrot. Well, at least he had got our attention for a bit.

I think Darren had a maturity well beyond his 23 years but he could be incredibly childish and irritating and he was the biggest hypochondriac I have ever met. He visited the doctor more than anyone else in the house and I always found it odd how his life-threatening illnesses occurred just before we were due to do a task!

I also had to admire the way he was always dressed up for the camera. He wouldn't even have a conversation unless he looked good for the viewers at home. His nickname in the house was 'the Count' (and that's not a spelling mistake), as he would always put his dark glasses on as soon as he got up.

The one occasion Darren and I really fell out was when I jokingly said that, because he had a nice car and dressed well, he must be a drug dealer. He went mad but you couldn't really joke about anything at Darren's expense because he always liked to be the one who looked cool.

I couldn't believe how incredibly sycophantic Darren was towards the girls – he was always cooking them little treats like banana fritters, which everyone else called the 'dog biscuits'. I'm surprised he didn't organise coffee mornings with them. The only time I ever really bonded with Darren was when we were both told off for looking over the wall towards Canary Wharf.

Mel
(The Praying Mantis)

My first impressions of Mel were that she looked like a tiny, lost child. I expected someone from *Big Brother* to come running into the house and tell us that there'd been a terrible mistake and the little girl's mum had come to collect her. But, unfortunately, that was not to be. Initially, Mel was incredibly quiet and for the first three days she really hung back, just observing what was going on. Little did she know that I was observing her even more than she realised. I had the added advantage that I didn't fancy Mel at all. She is the complete opposite of the women I'm attracted to, so I wasn't drawn into her web the way the rest of the poor suckers were. Even though the others nicknamed her 'the Feisty One' I always thought of her as the 'Praying Mantis' or 'the Black Widow', because she confided in me that she had once driven a boyfriend to suicide. I could well believe it. She flirted outrageously with all the men. I could actually see her calculating which of us would be of the most value to her. And all of the men she had liaisons with were booted out. What Mel was particularly good at was exposing people's weaknesses and she tried hard not to reveal anything about herself. When she realised how much Sada and Caroline infuriated us men she was very quick to ingratiate herself with us. She did this by taking her clothes off in front of us and I have to admit, even I was impressed by that.

If you ever asked Mel a straight question, her reply was always shrouded in psychobabble and, even though she was trying to come across as a trendy youngster (to appeal to the younger members of the audience, I thought) with her piercings and tattoos, the fact was she was a 28-year-old woman who still lived at home with her mum.

I think that Mel certainly has all the makings of a professional spy. That is, if her mum will let her out for the night. And I certainly think she would find it very easy to be a double agent. There was one very memorable moment when she upset Tom by getting him to admit that his father was very draconian, which I think proved that she had a very cruel streak. And I certainly think her degree in psychology helped her to stay in the house so long. But the strangest thing about Mel was what she brought into the house with her. I know certain people brought odd things in (Sada, her juggling balls; Tom, his book on astronomy; Caroline, herself), but Mel brought in a long plastic pipe that whistled when you swung it around your head. Odd, eh? But, then again, she could've used it as a blowpipe.

Sada
(Skeletor)

Ah, Sada, so beautiful, so talented, so interesting, so dim. I got the impression that the production team would have liked Sada and I to get a bit cosier than we did. You know the thing – nice posh girl cops off with nice posh boy. It would be a marriage made in heaven with a wedding list at Harrods. Imagine how gorgeous the kids would be, especially if they got their dad's looks and, er, their dad's brain. But it was never to be, I'm afraid, because apart from not being my type at all (far too bony – everyone in the house used to call her Skeletor), all she ever droned on about were three things: her fabulous boyfriend, the book she was writing and bloody tofu.

Now, you would think the conversations you could have about tofu would be pretty limited, what with it being, er, whatever it is. But no. Sada would ramble on and on about its magical properties. According to her, if everyone on the planet ate tofu, the world would be a better place. There'd be no more wars, famine or nasty people and we'd all live happily ever after. Sada went on so much about tofu that *Big Brother* gave her some as a present, which obviously didn't go down well with the rest of the group, especially us carnivores.

And meal times with Sada were always fun, especially when she insisted that we wait for her to sit down and say grace before we started to eat.

To be fair, when we first moved into the house, she was so different from anyone that any of us had encountered before she became an object of fascination. The girls, in particular, were really taken with her because, as they came from such completely different backgrounds, there is no way they would have met in the outside world. And she was writing a book which was all about men (a subject on which any group of women will bond).

Even though Sada tried to play down her privileged upbringing, the girls were fascinated by her chanting, her yoga and her singing. She even taught the girls a song which she said had been taught to her by a mystic. (Mystic Meg, if you ask me, as her singing left a lot to be desired.) But I think everyone started to realise that she was two lumps of tofu short of a vegetarian meal, the day she asked for a tortoise.

As you probably know, each week we were allowed to spend a certain amount of money on food. Weeell, sensible Sada thought it would be a good idea to buy a tortoise for the garden. When I pointed out to her that we would then be a bit short of food and may have to eat the tortoise, she exploded and started on one of her, 'we humans are horrible and we should be kind to the ickle creatures' rants. Oh, and we should eat more tofu. (The only way I would have eaten tofu at that stage is if it had been in the shape of a tortoise.) Even the girls were against her after that and really started to take the mickey out of her by changing the words to her mystic song and her chants.

Now, if there's one thing you shouldn't do, it's take the mickey out of Sada. Humour is not one of her strong points. Even though she thought she had a much more highly-developed sense of humour than anyone else in the house she never made anyone in the house raise even a chuckle. Sada also thought that she was really intelligent. This is like Peter Beardsley thinking he's a bit of a looker. And to prove how clever she was, the week before she came into the *Big Brother* house she appeared on Kilroy defending blonde girls against people who thought them stupid. Fair play to her, I say, but when we were working out how much time each of us could spend in the shower, considering it was only on for an hour a day, Sada vehemently insisted that we could have ten minutes each! (There were ten of us.) I don't think it's blondes who aren't clever, I think it's tortoise-loving tofu eaters.

As the first week wore on, it started to become obvious that Sada couldn't really hack it and all she talked about was how she wanted to leave, which made a change from her other boring topics of conversation, so it came as no surprise when she was voted out. It was then I realised that although this was a game show, I wanted to win it.

Tom
(The Quiet Man)

I didn't even realise that Tom was in the house at first because he was so quiet. Whereas everyone else was running around trying to get themselves noticed, Tom really held back and just watched what was going on. I later found out this was because he was very worried that we wouldn't be able to understand his Irish accent and it's true that, for the first couple of days, our only words to Tom were 'What?' This drove him even further into his shell.

I was actually a bit worried about Tom – well, not that worried, as he was the enemy as far as I was concerned, but I did tell Andy that if anyone was going to walk, it would probably be Tom. I decided to try to get him to come out of himself a bit more (I do believe it helps if you know your opponent) so I got him involved in a game of Cheat and funnily enough, he was surprisingly good at it.

Little by little, he started to come more and more out of his shell but he was morose and very serious as he was under a lot of pressure to return to his family's farm which he lived on with his dad and six sisters. As we got used to his accent, Tom became more and more confident and I was starting to like him a great deal but it used to infuriate me the way he would just lie down and accept the way his life was going and didn't try to change it at all. He didn't seem to bring anything to the group, either. He didn't cook, and I got the impression that he was spoiled at home by his sisters. I soon realised that Tom was the deepest member of the house and I can honestly say that, out of all of them, he was my favourite. He's also gone on record to say that he thinks I'm a genius so he's obviously a very bright lad with good taste too. I think the reason he lasted so long in the house was that, in the beginning, the audience also didn't really know he was there either.

And when he was nominated, it was me who encouraged him to go into the diary room and argue against it. And, of course, he was very good-looking, although I only realised that after I left the house and started reading what girlies thought of him. Tom was definitely attracted to Mel but she obviously thought that Andy was a better bet and tried hard at all his tasks. Yeah, nice one, Mel.

I was glad that Tom got as far as he did. And I think that the bright lights of London may have turned his head. He confided in me that he had never travelled so, hopefully for him, that's what he'll do next and not end up spending the rest of his life on a farm in Ireland.

Big Brother

I got the impression that once the show was up and running, *Big Brother* didn't really know how to handle it. It was as if they were the least prepared. They were always telling us that they had our best interests at heart, but this was obviously not true and, after all, they did have a television show to produce and they had to make it as interesting as possible no matter what the cost to us.

Big Brother would never answer our questions directly. If we had any queries, they would always tell us that they'd get back to us but would never give us a specified time. They would also contradict themselves regularly, most memorably when the told us not to feed the chickens potato skins. They retracted this when the vet told them that that was exactly what we should be doing.

We got to know the voices of *Big Brother* and to anticipate who would be on duty so we could go and have a chat with our favourite voices. The girls all preferred the men's voices while the boys preferred the women's. Thank heavens Caroline wasn't one of *Big Brother*. Imagine her voice waking you up in the morning – you'd be straight over the fence.

Big Brother were very unreasonable about

small things, like giving us enough hot water, and since watching the show, I've realised that it was edited to make a good programme and not to show what was really going on. Could *Big Brother* have edited the footage so as to change viewers' opinions of the people in the house? Well, they certainly had their own game plan.

Part Two

You Wanna Live Like Nasty Nick, You Gotta Think Like Nasty Nick

Are You a Complete and Utter Bastard Like Nick? Do This Quiz and Find Out.

1. You accidentally kill your granny's much-loved budgie Sparky when you're using it as a cricket ball. Do you ...

a. Nip down the pet shop, buy her a new budgie and break the news to her gently.

b. Put the brown-bread bird back in the cage and tell Granny that it passed away peacefully in its sleep.

c. Stick a hamster on Sparky's perch. When Granny questions why her beloved feathery friend is now a fat-cheeked rodent, tell Granny she's going mad and she'd better give you all of her money now before she pegs it and leaves her fortune to a rescue centre for old budgies.

2. Your mate sets you up on a blind date. When you meet the girl you see that she could easily come first in a moose look-a-like competition. (And all the other entrants were real moose.) Do you ...

a. Treat the girl to a slap-up meal, no expense spared.

b. Take her to a McDonald's and hope no-one sees you.

c. Tell Moosey you're just nipping to the loo, climb out of the window, go round to your mate's girlfriend's, give her a right good seeing to, tell her you're going to the loo, climb out of the window, nip around to your mate's mum's house, give her a right good seeing to, get her to cook you a slap-up meal and give you your cab fare home.

3. Your best mate confides in you that he has a blow-up rubber doll and uses it regularly. Do you ...

a. Explain to your pal that you admire his adult views on sexuality and tell him that you, too, will be buying a rubber friend.

b. Go straight down the pub and tell every one about his 'perversion'.

c. Break into his house. Hide in his wardrobe. Video your mate in action with his rubber lover. Put the movie on the Internet and charge everyone five quid a hit to see it.

4. A giant genetically-altered monster woman is terrorising the earth. Do you ...

a. Work with scientists trying to find a way to stop her reign of terror.

b. Offer to strap bombs to your body and sacrifice yourself for the sake of humankind.

c. Shag her senseless.

5. Which of these TV programmes would you like to present?

a. *How To Be The Perfect Parent*

b. *So You Want To Be Good At DIY*

c. *The Driving Fast Cars, Picking Up*

Scantily-Clad Women Who Will Go At It Hammer And Tongs In A Hot Lesbian Lovin' Type Of Way While You Join In And You Get To Fire Big Guns House Party.

6. Your mum knits you an awful jumper for Christmas. Do you ...

a. Wear it with pride – it's just what you've always wanted.

b. Keep it hidden in a drawer and only wear it when she comes to see you.

c. Swap the jumper for a giant ray gun and take over the world.

7. You are offered one million pounds to take part in a bare knuckle fight with an opponent of your choice. Who would you choose to fight?

a. Mike Tyson

b. Vinnie Jones

c. Lorraine Kelly

8. You're at a party and there's a girl there who doesn't fancy you.. Do you ...

a. Admire her for her for her strength of character.

b. Assume she's a lesbian.

ell her you're a multi-millionaire, you've only got a week to live and your dying wish is to lose your virginity to a woman as gorgeous as her and if she sleeps with you, you will leave her all your cash, your chocolate mountain and your collection of lovely puppies, kittens and ponies.

9. You're girlfriend tells you she's pregnant. Do you ...

a. Tell her that's just what you've always wanted and you should both get married straight away.

b. Go down the pub, get completely hammered and tell all your mates that you've been trapped.

c. Have plastic surgery, move to Thailand and open a string of lap-dancing bars.

10. Your brother and his wife have just had their first baby. And are having a party for your family to celebrate the birth. When you see the tiny cherub for the first time, do you ...

a. Burst into tears and tell them how lucky they are to be blessed with such a perfect little bundle of joy.

b. Have a quick glance and politely decline the offer to hold the stinky little parcel.

c. Arrive really drunk and tell everyone at the party that you're the real dad and have the video to prove it.

If you scored mostly:

As

Drop this book now. Put on some women's clothes, go outside and run up and down in the street shouting, 'Oooh, look at me I'm a right big girl and I fancy Christopher Biggins!'

Bs

As above.

Cs

Congratulations – you're well on the way to being a complete and utter bastard. Keep it up!

Women

NASTY NICK: HOW TO BE A RIGHT BASTARD

The thing about women is that they like being lied to. It's in their genes. Imagine if you told them the truth all the time. Their little brains couldn't take it. All those facts in that tiny space would fill it up pretty quickly and they wouldn't be able to think about the important things in life like wearing sexy underwear and cooking your dinner. Preferably at the same time.

Men have lied to women since time began. Adam probably told Eve, 'Of course her bum doesn't look fat in that fig leaf,' although, to be fair, he didn't have anything to compare it with and, if Eve had a sister, Adam would have certainly tried to convince them that a three-in-a-bed sex session reduces bum size by 50 per cent. I think my old housemate Andy would've made a perfect Adam. As all of us men know, the three-in-a-bed-sex-bum-reducing-thing really works . And it works faster the more women you get involved. It's a fact and has been proved by scientists – bloke scientists with really big brains packed full of clever things like equations and algebra and you can't argue with that stuff.

So if any of you girls are asked by your bloke to 'bring a friend', he's only helping you to look after your figure and is not a 'filthy pervert', so stop it with the tears, the shouting, scratching and biting.

Now, I've always had great success with women, but even you ugly blokes can cop off with top tottie if you just follow Nick's dating rules:

1. Never tell the truth to a woman – ever. How will she ever find out that you're not a jet fighter pilot who does charity work in his spare time? Who is she going to ask?

2. Never introduce a woman to your friends. Who knows, they might actually let slip that you get airsick. This is not something that top pilots tend to suffer from and even she may get a tad suspicious. What you should do is employ actors to pretend to be your friends (the better-looking the girl, the more actors you should employ. And I'm sure you can claim the expense back on your tax). That way you are sure to get glowing recommendations from all of your 'mates'.

One word of warning – be very careful in choosing your actors. Tom Cruise, for instance, would be a very bad choice as you

may find your new-found love waltzing out
the door with him. Go for the ugly character
actor type, such as, Eli Wallach or Old Man
Steptoe. This ensures that you will be the best
looking man in the room.

3. Never take a woman back to your place.
First of all, she will then know where you live.
This is very bad, especially if you don't want
your bunnies boiled. (I am, of course, talking
metaphorically here. You don't really have to
have bunny-wunnies unless it is an aid to
seduction.) And, of course, you are bound to
live in a hovel. One funny thing about women
is that they very rarely appreciate the aes-
thetic properties of a floor awash with lager
cans and pizza boxes. And they will certainly
frown on your 'specialist' magazine and video
collection.

No, the best thing to do in the event of a
woman wanting to see where you live is hire
somewhere. Preferably a show home. But
don't make it too flash. It still has to have that
'little-boy-lost, will-you-please-look-after-me'
look.

4. Always stop to pat a dog or give a baby some coochie coo. Women love to see the sensitive side of a man. If, however, she suggests maybe to get a dog or, worse still, have a baby, point up into the air and shout, 'My God what's that?' When she looks up, leg it.

5. Tell her your parents live in Africa. Well, do you want her meet them? Mums are women, too, and they managed to trap your dad so they know exactly what you are up to. And, as we all know, mums can read minds. Especially yours.

6. Always tell a woman that you hate football. That way, they'll think they'll have you all to themselves every Saturday. (Unfortunately, that's the day you do your charity work. I do mine at Fulham.) And beware women who say they enjoy the game. This is purely a ploy to trap men. One moment you're discussing the selection of the England team, the next you'll be in B&Q picking out bathroom tiles.

7. Dress to impress. Spend as much as you can't afford on clothes. Women like a well-turned-out man. And if you can only afford one outfit, this means you can only go on one date. Unless the outfit is reversible. If it is, on the other hand, you will never get a date in the first place as you will be too busy standing on train station platforms writing down numbers.

8. Have a bath.

9. Women like nice restaurants, so take her to the best you can afford. Any restaurant with the word 'Happy', 'Harvester', or 'Mc ...' in its name is not an option.

10. Try and be good in the sack. Always use protection. Apart from the fact that you could catch a myriad of diseases, she could get pregnant. If that happens, I suggest you try to change you blood group. Don't be selfish in your good lovin'. Remember, there's two of you. And the better you are, the more likely she is to tell her pals that between the sheets

you're like an acrobatic donkey. I guarantee they'll be wanting to give you a road test. And afterwards, on no account run screaming out of the room shouting, 'I can't wait to tell all my mates I've done it with a lady.' Give her a little cuddle and a phone number. Yes, I did say a phone number – on no account give her your real number.

Now, talking about women, you may have noticed the blokes in the house using words to describe the opposite sex you'd never heard before. Well, I can proudly say that I've made up my own language to describe some of the ladies I've met in the past. Learn the terms, and I guarantee they'll come in handy. Of course, if you're a woman, just substitute men.

The Language

Use this language wisely, my children.

Sharnagga
A Sharnagga is a woman who scores between 7 and 10 on a scale of 1–10.

Sharhala
A Sharhala is a woman who scores between 5 and 7.

Woohara
A Woohara is a woman who scores below 5.

Chingingway
A Chingingway is a Sharnagga below the age of 20.

After ten pints a Sharhala becomes a Sharnagga, but a Woohara is always a Woohara.

You'll find yourself slipping into these terms easily and you'll certainly keep yourself out of trouble and, hey, now you're bi-lingual without having to resort to all that listen-and-repeat nonsense.

The Mobile Phone

The mobile phone is surely the greatest invention of the twentieth century. Yeah, I know, planes, rockets and penicillin have all come in handy, but I'm writing the book, OK?

What a fantastic aid to modern living that little bundle of wires is. How else could we all let each other know that, 'I'M ON THE TRAIN.' I love shouting that little snippet of information down my phone even when I'm not on a train, just to see people's faces. I recommend it wholeheartedly, as well as using your 'miracle millennium mouthpiece' to phone women and tell them that you're 'on the way' (by train, obviously). Little do they suspect that what you actually mean is that you'll be on the way some time next week. ('You know what the trains are like, darling. Got any beer?')

Try and use it to wind people up as much as possible. Look at the effect my little phone joke had on Fleet Street. It sent them in to the type of frenzy that hasn't been seen since the days of 'Who killed JR?'

If you're travelling by plane, why not tell the woman with the noisy baby sitting next to you that you're just going to make a phone call and hope it won't disturb her darling cherub's crying? Watch as the colour drains from her face as you try to order an imaginary pizza while cruising at 50,000 feet. Then sit back and enjoy your flight as the woman and the screaming baby move to a different seat as she is now convinced that your phone call will cause the wings to fall off. How moving seat would save them in the event of a plane crash is beyond me. Oh, and that thing about the wings falling off if you use a mobile on a plane is absolutely true and don't forget to end your conversation with, 'I'M ON THE PLANE.' Variety, you see, it's the spice of life.

Use the phone in the cinema to tell all of your friends about the film you're watching or, better still, why not plant a mate in the cinema, ring him and have a long chat about what you'll be doing afterwards? Hey, imagine if you were watching a Western you could shout, 'HE'S ON THE PLAIN.' I have to stop typing here, as I'm laughing so much. What if the movie was about a plumber, you could shout, 'HE'S DOWN THE DRAI ...' Sorry.

The library is surely the perfect environment for the mobile. All that quiet. Not natural, is it? Actually you don't even have to take your phone out of your pocket. Just stand up and start shouting but make sure you're holding your hand up to your mouth pretending you're using the smallest mobile in the world. But don't forget to use 'I'M ON THE TRAIN' as this will ensure no one dares approach you, what with you obviously being a raving lunatic (although you may get a few threatening shushes).

What about using your phone at a music gig? Picture the scene: the lights dim, the dry ice is flowing, Chris De Burgh walks to the mike, the whole audience holds its breath in anticipation. 'Never seen you looking so good as you do toni ...'

'I'M ON THE TRAIN!'

Ah, my life would be complete.

My all-time favourite use of the mobile is in the theatre. Make sure you have your phone set on the loudest ring and get a mate to call you. Keep up a running commentary on how bad the play is and, in particular, how bad the acting is. I think you'll all get a better performance out of the actors and, no doubt, the whole audience will thank you (although they may chase you all the way to the station to express their gratitude. And when you get on the train ... well, you know the form.)

Why don't you experiment with your own

annoying use of the phone? If any of your friends leave theirs lying around, why not change the language on it? They'll enjoy the challenge of getting their phone back to it's normal English settings and you'll enjoy watching them throwing it across the room.

Remember, when using a mobile in public, shout as loud as possible – everyone else is genuinely interested in your private life ...

Around the House

You probably noticed that we did a bit of DIY around the house when we first moved in. OK, I know this involved certain people taking their clothes off, covering themselves in paint and pressing their naked bodies against the wall, but what would you rather see – naked women running around covered in vinyl silk or that dreadful bloke off changing *Changing Rooms* (Lawrence Llewellen-Blah de blah) rambling on about paint finishes? Exactly. I would go for the naked woman option every time. And you may remember there was something there for the ladies as Craig, Darren and Andy got their kit off, too. I, however, preferred to hang back as I thought this was all a desperate attempt at vote winning. Tom, of course, was nowhere to be seen.

But getting back to DIY, a pastime I try to avoid at any cost. Well, have you ever been in one of those DIY superstores? They're full of stunned-looking men who can't quite grasp just why they're there. But if you look carefully, there is usually a woman in the background enthusing about the colour of bathroom tiles. Don't worry, I'm not having a go at women here. I know how pathetic men are when it comes to making our habitat liveable. And if we weren't goaded along every now and again we would be quite happy to live in a house with one item of furniture – a fridge to keep beer in. Men may be quite happy to live in a pigsty for a bit but, after a while, we do long for a bit of comfort.

If there aren't any women spurring the men on, beware. Any loose males wandering around one of those stores will, without fail, be DIY buffs and are to be avoided at all costs as they will certainly know grommet, rawlplug and washer sizes for every bit of DIY that has ever been done. And they will no doubt try and tell you about it. Their stories of 'jobs around the house they have tackled' will resemble the tales of old soldiers reminiscing about the time they spent in the trenches. Although I'm sure the DIY stories will involve more blood, swearing and heroics. No doubt they were even presented with a medal after the time they fearlessly and without regard for their own safety decorated the spare room.

Wouldn't you just love to see a movie called *Saving Private Ryan So He Could Go Home And Fit Dormer Windows*? Well, maybe not.

I'm always amazed at how, with no training at all, certain men will attempt to transport a whole bathroom to another part of the house on a whim. Although this will invariably involve the bath ending up in the living room. Most blokes wouldn't be too worried about this, as it would mean they could have a bath and watch television at the same time. And with their beer fridge close by, they'd be in bloke heaven. I can't see the point of changing something just for the sake of change. Fair enough if you have no central heating – put some in – but get people who have some experience of doing it to have a go. If your only experience of plumbing is turning on a tap, my advice to you is leave well alone. In fact, my advice to you is live in a house that needs no work done to it at all. Preferably one fitted with cameras that broadcast your every movement to the nation. I guarantee, after you've been in a house like that, you'll be able to afford as many builders as you like.

Big Issue Sellers

GET A JOB! BUY A HOUSE!

Oh, come on, it's a joke. Just because someone has nowhere to live doesn't mean they have no sense of humour. Some of my best friends are, well, wealthy stockbrokers actually, but that's not the point. I have seen homeless people around, well, where else would they be? I always buy *The Big Issue*. At least the vendors have some sort of plan and are trying to get themselves off the streets and into a house. I would recommend that the house they get into does not contain Caroline or Nichola. Trust me, a subway is a far less risky option.

These People Are
Wasting Our Money!

When I was caught trying to win the game that we were playing, i.e. attempting to have most of the others evicted thus giving me more chance of winning the £70,000, I thought everyone realised that's exactly what it was – a game.

So I was astounded by the reaction my tactics got. Everyone in the media denounced me. Heaven forbid the media would ever use any underhand tactics, eh? Apparently, even the Queen Mum said she was going to come round my house and give me a right good kicking. That last bit may not have been strictly true, but you get my gist.

But what struck me as I read the papers and caught up with all the news I had missed while I had been housebound, was, compared with what some people get up to, I have behaved like Mother Superior, The Pope and Bonnie Langford in a 'Who Can Be The Nicest?' competition. (I'd put my money on Langford – I've met her. She's so nice your teeth hurt).

Name me a politician you think you can really trust. Exactly. Now that puts it all into perspective, doesn't it?

For instance, what about that lot who built the Millennium Bridge? Talk about trying to talk your way out of a situation. At least I put my hands up and admitted it.

Never in my life have I seen such a bunch of slippery characters than those blokes trying to explain why the Millennium Bridge is bouncing around like a snake in a tumble drier. And, of course, they insist it's not their fault. How could it be? I mean they're only bridge-building experts – they were probably off bridge-building school the day they were teaching 'bouncy bridge'. The best excuse I heard was that they didn't expect to have large groups of people walking across it. Well, you wouldn't would you, what with it being a pedestrian bridge? That's like airlines telling us that the reason planes are dropping out of the sky, is because of those pesky passengers that insist on getting on the aircraft and going on their holidays to enjoy themselves.

Now, this bridge cost us 18 million quid! That's a heck of a lot of folding stuff! It would have been cheaper and safer to have the bridge boffins give everyone a piggyback to the other side of the river, than to waste all that money on what is basically, is a long bouncy castle. Imagine what we could spend eighteen million quid on? Daft things like hospital beds or operations or research into disease. Mind you, the bridge-building blokes would probably tell us that it's pointless spending money to help people, because those horrible people would probably turn up and this would mean nothing would work and it certainly wouldn't be their fault because they've got a note from their mum.

Now, what I want to know is how they got it so wrong? We have computers that can simulate everything from the trajectory of satellites around the Earth to how many fat blokes you can get into an industrial spin-drier. So, did none of these highly-paid 'bridge-building' buffoons think to do some sort of test to see what happens when people tramp across it with their size nines? Although, to be fair, a lot of those people were children and, as we know, children put a completely different spin on any scientific experiment – that's why NASA don't send kids into space. It's to do with, er, weight or sweets or something.

Now, I've got a really good idea – why don't we just sell the Millennium Bridge for scrap; we could even stick the Dome in there as well – we'd probably get a couple of bob for that. With the money we could get some boot-building boffins to build a giant robotic boot and then we could charge people to wear the giant robo-boot and kick the arses of the bendy bridge-building blokes through London. I guarantee it would be a bigger attraction than the Millennium wheel.

Driving

It has been said that driving a car is one of man's greatest pleasures. I don't know who actually said this. Probably that big curly-headed fellow who's always on the telly talking about engines and tyres and such like in that 'stop-start' way he does. But he does seem to know what he's talking about, so we'll give him the benefit of the doubt. I have to say that after 'Ladies Beach Volleyball', driving features prominently in my life and I do thoroughly enjoy it, especially if the car I'm driving has the word Porsche or Ferrari somewhere on the bodywork. And thanks to *Big Brother*, these sort of cars now feature regularly in my life.

But remember, driving can kill, especially if you get stuck behind some doddery old fool and their caravan. You could die of boredom sitting there watching night turn to day then summer into autumn as you try and inch your way past them. Or go mad with road rage and try to run them off the road. And that will happen when you realise that you have a life and you want to be getting on with it.

Now I know that caravaners get a lot of bad press but quite frankly, they deserve every single bit of it. And which genius first thought, 'Look, there's a brand, spanking new motorway open. You know what it needs now? A house on wheels trundling up and down. We could get a whole load of them together. That would be perfect, just what that new road needs.' And while I'm on about the 'transportable living space that dare not speak it's name' ...

Q: What is the collective noun for a bunch of caravans on the motorway?

A: A graveyard.

Although I'm not sure that's strictly true, because compared to a caravan, graveyards can corner like they're on rails and they're much faster.

Which is just how I like to move. Faster. Well what's the point of having a car that'll go from nought to next week in a millisecond and then not be able to put your foot down because you're stuck behind a mobile house?

I think you should only be allowed to tow a caravan if you've been convicted for speeding. How embarrassing would that be for all those boy racers with their souped-up Astras and Fiestas to be sentenced to three months towing a rusty caravan behind them? The only thing it would say on their windscreen then would be 'Billy-no-mates'.

And on the subject of boy racers, I seem to meet a lot more of them now, usually at traffic lights. My car seems to attract them and repel them at the same time as they zoom straight up to me, their arm out of the window, then try and get away from me as fast as they can.

I do like to wind them up by following them for a while. This is usually quite easy, as having go-faster stripes and a big exhaust does not necessarily make your car go faster, whereas having a powerful engine in a lightweight body usually does the trick.

If I do lose them, they're quite easy to locate due to the volume of their car stereos. I could never understand how they could possibly get the music to be so loud, then I found out that they actually have them customised at the cost of thousands of pounds to throw out thousands of watts. Why? If they want to listen to music that loud why not go to a nightclub? Who knows, they might meet a girl, or get some friends.

I've been meeting lots of new friends recently and it's all down to my driving. Well, not exactly my driving, more my parking. It's funny how the simple action of parking a car – especially a bright red car with a prancing horse motif – can attract all sort of admirers. I tend not to bother with the ones who want to know what the brake horsepower is or how many miles to the gallon I get. But I do like to have a chat with the ones who are giggling and who seem to be wearing the least amount of clothes they can without getting arrested. I am talking about women here; the thought of seeing some blokey car buff in a pair of silver hot pants doesn't bear thinking about.

I've had some fascinating conversations about, er, cars with some very interesting 'enthusiasts' and it's all down to *Big Brother*. Well, that and my game plan.

Driving II

I was trying to move on and write some new stuff here but I had a nagging feeling it wasn't just caravan owners who got on my nerves. I knew there was someone else on our roads that drove me mad. Then it suddenly hit me (and I'm surprised they haven't already, their driving skills are so bad) when I was stuck in traffic this morning and late for a meeting. Of course! People carrier and four-wheel-drive jeep drivers, the latter being a vehicle that is so handy for the hilly terrain of Fulham, which is where I live at the moment.

As soon as anyone has a child, they believe that the whole world is geared to them. Especially if they're middle-class. Whereas working-class parents just seem to get on with it and the kids grow up to be perfectly normal. This is the same with really posh parents who are quite happy to let their kids eat mud and take gigantic horses over fences while firing shotguns. Certainly no molly-coddling for them. It's always the middle-class parents who seem to wrap their kids in cotton wool and can't believe that their darling offspring could possibly venture out of the house without being eaten by a shark. And this is where the people carrier or jeep comes in. You see, they need to be as high up and have as much metal as possible between them and the other cars who are dying to run them and their darling child into a blazing ditch full of crocodiles.

Now, the thing is that Mummy used to drive a Nissan Micra and all of a sudden they're behind the wheel of a jeep with a jet engine, or a people carrier, which to them is like driving an articulated lorry. This is why they drive so slowly and cause tailbacks of up to 100 miles. They also think they can stop wherever they like whenever they like to have pointless conversations with people driving similar vehicles, blissfully unaware of the mayhem they are causing. After all, their child is much more important than any silly little accident going on behind them. They're scared that if they drive their big shiny new kid transporter properly, they could take off and end up on the moon and everyone knows that's a dangerous place for little Sophie or Tarquin to be. What with there being no oxygen or crêches or nannies or anything.

So, if you do own one of the aforementioned vehicles and you live in the city, could you sell it, buy a caravan and go live in the country? Your little darling would be safe there.

Look, I just had to get that off my chest.

Music

One of the worst things about being in the house was that we weren't allowed to have any music. Well, OK, we did have Caroline with her sax and Anna with her guitar, but they're not exactly Steps, are they? And, as you know, every time Caroline started wailing away, I always took steps to get as far away from her as I could. Although the racket she made did come in handy for drowning out any conversations I didn't want overheard. It also drowned out the helicopters that were always circling overhead.

I really missed having music as I have it playing continually either on my Walkman or on my CD player, no matter what I'm doing. From Barry White if I'm trying to get a bit romantic to Iron Maiden if I'm trying to sacrifice a virgin to a mutant robot or whatever it is that Maiden scream about. Oh, and I recommend that you don't get the two mixed up as I have personal experience that the Iron Maiden track 'Bring Your Daughter to the Slaughter' is not the best of tunes to slip on when you've invited someone back for coffee. The late-night sound of doors slamming and car engines being revved up can annoy your neighbours. It's never really advisable to play Iron Maiden when anyone else can hear it, anyway. But it's quite handy in emergencies, like if you're cleaning the toilet and need to give yourself a quick boost.

I've always had a very eclectic taste in music, much to the annoyance of my friends, as they can be subjected to anything from from Boney M to Bizet when they pay me a visit. I also have the annoying habit of buying an album just for one track and playing it continually. You certainly get to find out who your friends are then.

The Eighties was certainly my favourite era for pop. I'm still a big fan of The Bangles, Erasure, Bananarama and Dexy's Midnight Runners. And I have yet to see a band as exciting live as the original line up of Duran Duran.

The weird thing is that I have been getting offers to release a single! Now since I'm a firm believer that the music you make should reflect your musical taste, I don't really think the public are quite ready for the mixture of all the above influences. And what would I wear on Top of the Pops? Maybe a mixture of Eighties fashion. What a treat that would be for the licence-paying public.

My favourite place to listen to music is in the bath, preferably with some candles burning, a glass of cold white wine and a female friend. But there's one artist that I don't think I will be using again to set the mood on a cosy romantic evening and that's George Michael. This goes back to a conversation I was having when I was in the house. We were talking about George getting arrested in a toilet in America, and I said that I thought this could be a very dangerous thing to do in America where people carry guns. You never know how upset they could get, especially if there were any children around. George could've been filled full of lead.

Anna took this completely the wrong way and thought I was having a go at gays and suggesting they were all paedophiles which, of course, I wasn't (don't you just hate it when people are so politically correct it makes them blind to anyone else's point of view?). Well, wouldn't you just know it – George Michael was only watching the show and he sent word that everyone in the house was invited out for dinner except me. Oh well, I never liked Wham anyway.

Animals

You may remember me mentioning earlier that Big Brother once set us the exciting conversation topic of 'Which are better – cats or dogs?' Well, without doubt, it has to be dogs. How anyone can even allow a cat in the house is beyond me. Let's face it, cats can do absolutely nothing. I challenge all you cat owners to give me one example of a useful function that a cat can perform. Yes, they may sit on you purring but, as we all know, this is only blackmail so you'll feed them. And once you've filled them up with that dreadful fishy goo they're out of there, mate. And you don't exist until feeding time comes around again. That's unless they want to give you a nice present of, say, a decapitated bird or the bloody remains of a mouse. If that's the sort of thing you appreciate, then you and cats deserve each other.

I think my hatred of cats goes back to when I was a child. I lived in a big house and in the stables, apart from our three horses, lived eight cats which I wanted nothing to do with at all. I had my mind set on a much more exotic creature – I was fascinated by parrots.

I couldn't get enough of them. I'd cut their pictures out of magazines, get books about them out of the library, watch everything on TV that remotely featured a parrot – I wanted to be Long John Silver. You may remember a scene in the series *Robinson Crusoe* that seemed to be on every summer holiday, when Robinson finally taught his parrot to say his name. Well, I ran around the room punching the air after I'd watched that. What a fantastic bird! And apart from looking great, they could talk. I think this is what had fascinated me all along. Imagine having a pet that could talk back to you. Now that would be a pet worth having.

I pestered my parents for weeks begging for a parrot. They 'ummed' and 'aahed' and finally after much deliberation they got me a kitten! A kitten! I was outraged. What possible use could I have for a kitten? Can a kitten sit on your shoulder and shout pieces of eight? Can a kitten tell you where the pirate's treasure is buried? Of course it can't, and I should know because I tried my hardest to get it to do so, but it wasn't having any of it. It would just sit looking cute. A fat lot of good that would be on a desert island. I would've handed it straight over to the cat-eating cannibals. And to add insult to injury, my furry, mute ball-of-fluff was called Thomasina. It was a girl cat. How embarrassing. Don't worry, I looked after it. Well, I did until it discovered the delights of the barn and the other cats. Then I would only see her from afar running around trying to catch rats and mice.

It wouldn't surprise me to learn that cats can talk, but they're so sneaky they just don't talk to humans.

After my kitten-instead-of-parrot trauma, which I'm surprised I got over unscathed, I got a dog. I called her Samantha and from that day on I have been a confirmed dog-lover. What other animal gives you unconditional love and enables you to cop off with women when you're walking them in the park? You wanna get a girl, get a Labrador, that's my motto.

Unfortunately, I can't keep a dog now as I live in a flat, but I do have two goldfish called 'No' and 'Names'. They can't talk either. And the only conversation I'm likely to have if I take my fishy friends for a walk in the park is with the police.

There aren't many of God's creatures I dislike, but I'm not a big fan of rats or snakes. I've never liked rats because there were so many of them in the barn at home. What on earth were all those cats doing in there? Probably giving all the other animals elocution lessons. And I was once attacked by a snake in Australia. It was an Australian Black Snake, so called because it was a snake, it was black and it's from Australia. If there's one thing you don't do, it's mess around with the poisonous things that wander around in the bush in Oz. The spiders are big enough to carry weapons. Not that they'd need them, since all they have to do is look at you and you'll drop dead. And all that stuff about then being more scared of you than you are of them is absolute nonsense. The predators in Australia go out looking for trouble. Especially after a few tinnies.

I was really lucky in my snake encounter because it missed my flesh and sank its enormous, poison-dripping fangs into my boot. Needless to say, I was more scared of the snake than it was of me. My Australian companions thought the Pommie jumping around screaming was a great laugh. Well, just wait until they come to our country and a cat gives them the wrong directions or sells them the Tower of London.

I do love animals, though, and I regularly give a donation to the Save the Rhino Fund. I think it's a great shame that these majestic animals will one day be extinct. Out of all the shows I've been offered to present, I would love to host a show involving animals. Especially if it had something to do with conservation. Hey, I may have had a game plan concerning getting rid of humans but I have a more serious intent when it concerns protecting the other creatures on the planet.

Johnny Foreigner

Because I've travelled extensively, I find meeting people from other countries fascinating. I believe you can learn more from observing other people's cultures and customs first-hand than you could ever learn from books, television or film and my advice to any youngster reading this is, to get on the first plane outta here. In fact, this goes for anyone. It's the only way you're going to learn.

There are, of course, exceptions to the rule about learning from other countries and this is when that other country is America. Land of the free – home of the idiot. Don't get me wrong, I love America. It's just the dysfunctional natives I can't stand. And by 'natives' I don't mean the American Indian. You only have to drive through a modern reservation to see how past American governments have run them into the ground. I'm surprised more American presidents haven't been assassinated by bow and arrow.

The Yanks I mean are those big, fat, gun-carrying, the-rest-of-the-world-don't-mean-doodly rednecks who always seem to be blocking the pavements in the centre of London. And, no, it isn't called a 'sidewalk'! Who invented the language? I was fascinated to see that in the American version of *Big Brother* the contestants were offered bribes to leave the house. This was so the production team could introduce another contestant to spice things up a bit. To their credit, the housemates wouldn't take the bribe as they all wanted a go at winning the $500,000 prize money. But how boring must the show have been if the production company wanted someone out.

And what about American sport? How do they convince the spectators to sit through four hours of American football? I'll tell you how – by offering waitress service and supplying them with as much food and drink as they can take. I'm surprised they can move anywhere at all. But they usually do. Over to this country just in time to stand in front of me when I'm in a hurry.

And what about basketball? Well, I have two words – Dennis Rodman. Now David Beckham might wear Posh's knickers but at least he doesn't wear her dresses, make-up and jewellery which, if you've ever seen Rodman, you'll know is exactly his choice of attire. American kids are daft enough without using this clown as a role model.

There is an American singer called Marilyn Manson. He cleverly put together the name of two American icons. Marilyn Monroe and Charles

Manson, (I ask you – Charles Manson!) as part of his bad-boy image to convince the American record-buying public that he was a devil-worshipping, graveyard-living, vampire baby-eater. The Americans fell for it hook, line and sinker. He came over here to perform to British music fans and was laughed out of town. See what I mean? They're daft as brushes.

And what about guns? Americans still go on about the right to bear arms – a law that was passed to protect the early settlers and has nothing to do with drive-by shootings using an AK-47 or a Kalashnikov. But still they'll defend their right, even if it means shooting each other to get their point across.

And, finally, my biggest gripe of all – American beer.

Q: Why is American beer is like a canoe?

A: Because it's close to water.

Boom! Boom! My dog has no nose ... my wife's gone to the West Indies, etc, etc. Oh, and just in case you do think that I'm being a tad unfair to our American cousins, they have given us some things that I'm thankful for – there's *The Simpsons* and, er, well that's it really.

Fashion

Us Brits are, without doubt, the worst-dressed people in the world. You only have to spend sometime in Italy or France to see how dowdy we look. Which other nation could have invented the shell suit and worn it as if it was the height of sartorial elegance? It always struck me when I saw people wearing what is essentially a tracksuit how unathletic they looked. The only people who can beat us in the badly-dressed stakes are my old friends ... the Americans! Where do they get all the material to make those gigantic shorts they all wear? There must be textile factories all over America on full production just to keep up the creation of garish material so big, fat Americans can carry on their quest of blocking as many pavements in Europe as possible.

British men are very badly dressed and this is because we can't be bothered and leave all that dressing up stuff to everyone else. We didn't win two World Wars and a World Cup by dressing like a seventeenth-century fop.

I do have the perfect solution to our problem of the British football hooligan abroad, though. At each passport control there should be a fashion expert watching who's coming through, what they're wearing and searching their luggage. Anyone found in the possession of man-made materials, a big, fat tattooed beer belly that hangs over their cheap jeans, or if their shoes don't match their belts, they'd be out. Imagine the money saved on charming foreign cafés not getting their furniture smashed up. Surely it would run to millions. And we wouldn't have to endure the television coverage of bloated, sweaty British blokes whingeing on how it wasn't their fault and how someone else started it, as usual. Then watching someone from the government wearing an ill-fitting suit telling us all in their most caring voice that they're doing their best to stamp the violence out. My plan works for me.

Women are much better than men at selecting the perfect outfit for any occasion. And this always proves itself in the summer months when the sun peeps from behind the clouds and all the men in the country decide to slip into those shorts they last wore when they were snake-hipped teenagers. Cleverly combining the snug-fitting shorts with grey socks, brogues and a T-shirt with a witty slogan, ensures that the chubby chaps are instantly transformed once again into sweaty blokes wearing bad clothes. I really don't know how you ladies hold yourselves back. But – and this is what always gets me about you women – no matter what age, shape or size you girls are, at the first sign of a bit of warm weather you girls just skip to your wardrobe and, without even looking, grab something small and summery, throw it on and off you go into the sunshine. Listen, girls, can I just tell you that all of you look fantastic in the sunshine with your summery gear on. It cheers us blokes right up, so stop it with yer whingeing about, oh, you know, all those girly things – I don't have to tell you what they are. There are more embarrassing things than a bit of cellulite. Roller blades for instance, especially when the wearer is going backwards with a look of 'I'm great, me' plastered all over their smug face. Roller blades are a fashion item that should have been stamped out years ago.

But there's been a recent development in pedestrian transportation in the capital that makes even roller bladers look cool. Grown adults have taken to riding around the streets on scooters. And I don't mean the types that the Italians drive while sipping cappuccino and looking cooler than Clint Eastwood in a fridge, but the scooters we all had as kids until we realised how daft we looked.

Now, I suspect that this sudden outbreak of scooter mania was something to do with fashion. I think the shell suit manufactures were annoyed that they weren't making as much money as they were, so they decided to create another way of making everyone look daft and they came up with scooters for adults. They then stuck some pictures in a few style magazines and, hey presto, before you know it, the scooter is the thing to propel you around London.

Mind you, that's London and only London because if you rode a scooter anywhere else in the country you may get people trying to stuff you in a waste bin and set you on fire.

Now, I suppose scooters are good for the environment what with having no engine or anything but I'd rather have a bunch of pandas pulling me around on a skateboard than face the embarrassment of scootin'. But I reckon that if some trendy young upstart can start a craze, so can I. So I'm telling you – the trendy mode of transport to get you around the city is the Spacehopper; light, comfortable and environmentally friendly, and you still won't look as daft as a fat bloke on a scooter.

My Only Love

It's a bit difficult to write this bit as my co-author Mickey is in what can only be described as a huff, and is stamping his foot like the big girl that he is. He's even trying to wrestle me away from the computer screen so he can put his point of view to the world. But since I am a giant of a man at 6ft and he is the size of a bee it is quite easy to keep him out of reach of the keyboard and in his rightful place – the kitchen, making the tea and arranging the Hob Nobs.

The reason for all this fighting, shouting and tears (the tears are from him, not me) is quite simply football. You see, Mickey is a Geordie boy and believes that the only team worth mentioning are his beloved Newcastle United. But I have assured him in no uncertain terms that there is only one team I wish to have mentioned and that is my very own Fulham FC. And the more he shouts that I am a 'soft southern get', the more it strengthens my resolve to keep him as far away from this bit of the book as I can. And to tell you the truth, I have absolutely no idea what he is talking about most of the time anyway. Girls of my acquaintance assure me that the Geordie accent is very sexy, but to my refined ears it just sounds like a load of mixed-up vowels.

So, with a well-served cup of tea and a Hob Nob at my elbow, let's get on with it.

I first went to see Fulham in 1973 and have been watching them ever since. My support goes so deep that when I have a suit made, it is lined with the Fulham strip. (It takes three strips.) People are often quite stunned when they see the white lining of my jacket and the Number Three inside. What I really appreciate about Fulham is how well the supporters are treated unlike, say a team like Chelsea, who will find any excuse for hiking up the price of admission to their games. (I made sure it was put in my contract that I was allowed to knock Chelsea as much as I can.)

Fulham's supporters are some of the most loyal in the country and will be there through snow in Wigan, rain in Darlington and train delays to Lincoln and are the most good-natured supporters I've ever met. I would never have visited such exotic places as Hull, Carlisle or Bolton if it hadn't been for my beloved Fulham. And at all these places we are always treated well.

I'm sure that, in five years, Fulham will be a big club again, but I think that this will have its cost as the higher a club gets the less they seem to care about their fans. Mickey is shouting at me that Newcastle United give all their fans bags of jewels and free pies and mink-lined duffel coats to wear when it's cold but I think he's just trying to put me off. So my true love is Fulham FC because there is a passion in their playing, a passion in their fans and a passion in their players. You see, the Geordie boy couldn't have written anything as poetic as that.

What's On?

Television! I love it. I always have and I love it even more now that I'm on it. But I'm very choosy in what I watch. I can't just veg out in front of it. The programmes I watch have to be of a certain standard. A shiver still runs down my spine when I think of some of the dross I watched as kid. *Cheggers Plays Pop* or *John Craven's Newsround* were enough to send me running from the room. I'd rather spend time with the chatless Thomosina than watch that rubbish and now I can't stand the dreadful *Star Trek* especially *The New Generation*. Sorry, trekkies IT'S NOT REAL SO STOP DRESSING UP LIKE THEM – or any show involving decorating or gardening. If anyone can explain to me how on earth Lawrence Llewellin (needs a makeover himself) Bowen or Charlie (fat, saggy, can't string-a-sentence-together ginger bird) Dimmock got on television, can they please write it down and send it to me because I'd love to know. But thank God there's some good stuff on TV: *The Simpsons*, *Friends*, *Soccer AM*. I love watching the repeats of shows like *Bewitched* that was a favourite of mine when I was a kid. The only thing about it though, and it still puzzles me to this day, is why Darren was always stopping his wife Samantha from using spells. If I was married to a witch who could magic up anything I wanted, I'd never do another days' work ever.

Oh, and another one of my favourite re-runs is *The Addams Family*. Now, in their house there is a hand called Thing who will do little jobs around the house. It's a good job Thing wasn't around with Andy in the *Big Brother* house — poor old Thing would've been exhausted.

I loved the recent show *Queer As Folk*. Great acting and production values and it wound everyone right up. To anyone who was upset by it, I'd just like to say, 'This is real life, so stop watching reruns of *The Good Life*.' I was amazed to find out that my good pals the Americans had bought *Queer As Folk* but unsurprisingly, it has been reported in the British press that the channel showing it received a boycott from advertisers including Versace whose murdered chairman was openly gay and hang on, wasn't he a friend of George Michael? I hope George isn't inviting anyone from Versace out to dinner.

More Sport

Just because I'm a football fan and could watch it, in the words of George Michael, 'twenty-four, seven,' it doesn't mean that I'm a fan of every sport. Far from it. Some televised sports can have me running down the pub quicker than a *Best of Changing Rooms Special.*

Stuff like curling, bowls, rowing, horse racing, motor racing or any track event are so boring that I have to be woken up so I can get out of the house. Apart from football, there are loads of sports that should have far more coverage. What about the remarkable expertise exhibited in topless darts? Surely one of our most under-rated sporting pursuits and it's definitely a great shame it isn't classed as an Olympic sport. You can't tell me that the ancient Greeks didn't have something like that in the first Olympic games. They certainly didn't have synchronised swimming, but that seems to get in every four years. I do like to watch it though, just because it gives me a right laugh. Who thought it up? How did he get everyone else to take him seriously? How did he pitch it? Is there some big meeting when everyone gets together with their new sporting ideas to try and get them included in the Olympics? I can only surmise that on the day synchronised swimming was put forward, there must have been other ideas so ludicrous – things like panda tickling or monkey bouncing – that having a load of women swimming around doing exactly the same things wearing nose clips and forced smiles must have seemed like a good idea and it was in.

If *Changing Rooms* added another ingredient to their programme, something like boxing or wrestling, it would certainly decrease my alcohol consumption and I suspect some of the victims of their make-overs would like to get involved in the punching, kicking and gouging, too. Hey, how about a gladiatorial-type event with the team from *Changing Rooms* and the team from *Ground Force*. They could even build and decorate their own arena to save money. We could have an international event and bring TV make-over and gardening teams over from different countries.

I bet there's some television producer in a television production office high above us now, reading this and thinking, 'This is a great idea. Imagine the viewing figures!' I guarantee it. So if you see a new show called *Changing Rooms and Ground Force – A Fight to the Death!* you know where you read it first ...

Be Careful What You
Wish For - You Might
Get It

OK, so you want to be involved in television. You dream of being a star, the host of your very own *Supermarket Sweep*. It looks really glamorous, and it is, it's a fantastic life. But if you do get there, what you then have to do is sustain it and make sure everyone wants you again and again. What you really don't want to happen is the door to open and in the words of the Master, Jim Bowen 'Let's show you what you could've won,' have it cruelly slammed shut in your face. And there's loads that can go wrong.

And if the public stop liking you, it's over. Strangely, even though I was always portrayed as the bad guy in the press, the public have always been very nice to me. The majority of people I suspect would have done what I did. I would advise that you try and not to get yourself into the Sunday papers if the words under-age, drugs, floppy, vampire, chicken, voodoo or Anthea Turner appear in any story involving you – if they do, that's it, mate, you're finished. I always try to get involved in stories showing me to be a hero. Grabbing people from under the hooves of a galloping horse is always a good story, but that's quite hard to arrange. Even harder if you live in a high rise but it would certainly get you in the papers. Another unfortunate thing about being in the public eye is that you can't really trust anyone any more. Your old friends are fine, but it's very difficult to make new ones, especially if they're women.

Imagine you're out on a date with a demure young lady, only to find your picture splashed across the tabloids the next day and a story telling the world that, in actual fact, your date was a mud-wrestling, lap-dancing strip-o-gram who's trying to get on the telly and is looking for her big break – and you're it. I tell you, it happens ... er ... not to me but ... er ... someone I know. Everyone wants a piece of you and it's usually because they want to further their own career. So think twice before you decide to get involved in the TV game. It'll drive you mad. Actually, it'll drive you whereever you want to go because if you do make it, you'll have a chauffeur. Just hope that he's discreet.

Nick's Lists

(Well, I had to do something when I wasn't scheming ...)

House Favourites
1.   Tom
2.   Andy
3.   Sada
4.   Mel
5.   Craig
6.   Anna
7.   Darren
8.   Caroline
9.   Nichola

Top Babes
1.   Grace Kelly
2.   Lady Di
3.   Sharon Corr (violin player, The Corrs)
4.   Kate Jackson (Original Charlie's Angel)
5.   Suzannah Hoffs (lead singer, The Bangles)
6.   Tara Palmer-Tomkinson
7.   Carol Vorderman
8.   Lynda Carter (Wonder Woman)
9.   Gillian Anderson
10.   Julia Roberts

Top Older Tottie

1. Stephanie Beecham
2. Anna Ford
3. Selena Scott
4. Goldie Hawn
5. Jane Fonda
6. Barbara Bach
7. Sheena Easton
8. Andie McDowell
9. Linda Lusardi
10. Jet (Gladiator)

Top Geezers

1. Carl Foggerty
2. Eddie The Eagle
3. Sean Connery
4. Vinnie Jones
5. Clint Eastwood
6. Mel Gibson
7. David Niven
8. Billy Joel
9. Simon Morgan (cpt Fulham FC)
10. Tom Hanks

Top Ten Terrors

1. Jeremy Beadle
2. Jeremy Sprake
3. Andi Peters
4. The Gallagher Brothers
5. Peter Allis
6. Loyd Grossman
7. David Icke
8. William G Stewart
9. Paul Jones (Synergy FM, Bournemouth)
10. Bungle (Rainbow)

Top Ten Cartoons

1. *Dangermouse*
2. *Dogtanion and The Three Muskahounds*
3. *Batfink*
4. *Muren Bushstanzeiger*
5. *The Space Sentinels*
6. *Scooby Doo* (Original)
7. *Animal Crackers*
8. *Yogi Bear*
9. *Top Cat*
10. *Tom And Jerry*

The Most Boring Conversation Openers

1. How does it feel to be out of the house?
2. What are you doing here?
3. What's Mel really like?
4. Are you really that nasty?
5. You sound just like you do on telly.
6. Who's your favourite to win?
7. Who's your least favourite to win?
8. What are you going to do now?
9. Do you write your column in the *Sun*?
10. I hear you're going to present *The Big Breakfast*?

Top Ten Tottie Towns

1. Gothenburg
2. Copenhagen
3. Amsterdam
4. Belgrade
5. Talin (Estonia)
6. Manchester
7. Nottingham
8. Bath
9. London
10. Ramsgate

Top Ten Movies

1. *Kind Hearts and Coronets*
2. *It's a Wonderful Life*
3. *Life Is Beautiful*
4. *The Sting*
5. *There's Something About Mary*
6. *The Lavender Hill Mob*
7. *Live And Let Die*
8. *Four Weddings And A Funeral*
9. *The Gods Must Be Crazy*
10. *Marathon Man*

I Really Hate …

1. People who are rude to waiters
2. Milk cartons
3. Committee members of golf clubs
4. Early episodes of *Bod*
5. Keith Chegwin
6. Tube trains
7. Skegness
8. 'Cute' rings on mobiles
9. The radio ad for Brightco double glazing
10. The customer support team at Vodafone

The Aftermath

Well, now it's all over and we all know who won on that last wet Friday night in the house. While I think it's fanatastic that Craig won and how kind it was of him to donate his winnings to Joanne Taylor so she could have a heart-lung transplant, is there anyone else who thinks that the ending was just too perfect? The last three contestants were a black guy, a lesbian and a salt of the earth working class guy who gives the money away to save someone's life. If that's not a perfect ending tell me what is. I wonder who they'll get to play me in the film? Probably Danny Devito.

The Sunday following the end of the series there was an auction of memorabilia from the *Big Brother* house on Channel 4. I was determined to bid for the chair from the diary room and I was in contact all day as the bids rose. I took the bidding up to £25,000, it was all for a good cause and they told me I was bidding against a celebrity although they wouldn't tell me who it was. I thought this a bit unfair as they were broadcasting my bids. Then they just stoppped calling me and the chair went for £30,000.01p to one of my favourite comics Alan Davies. It's great that he got the chair and donated so much money to charity but odd that they stopped calling me. Were Channel 4 still trying to portray me as Nasty Nick? Well, it's good publicity after all.

That Sunday also saw Nichola perform her new single for the first time on TV. It was dreadful. I think that was a good lesson to anyone wanting to get in the business not just to take anything anyone offers just to be on TV.

There's been so much written in the press about us all, some of it was even true. And many copy cat shows have followed. I'm glad I was involved in the first show of its type, and amazed it had the whole nation glued to their screens.

Even now, people are still fascinated by *Big Brother* and approach me all the time to ask questions about my experience in the house. What I have learned is that this can be great fun but you have to be up for it. If it's a cold, wet Wednesday and you're not looking your best, the last thing you want is to be collared by someone wanting to know your life story. I try to be polite at all times because, even though I may have heard the public's questions a million times before, it is probably the first time that person has ever had the chance to ask it.

I have also been let down badly by people who've used me purely for publicity and people who have promised me things that have never materialised. One of my biggest disappointments was when I checked up on the archive material on the Internet. I was amazed at how biased they had been towards me, always highlighting my bad points and mentioning my good points in a very sarcastic manner. On the other hand, Darren is always talked of in glowing terms. Does his mum work there or something.

OK I'll stop whingeing now. I'm once again trying to warn anyone who wants to get into this business how hard it can be especially if people take against you. And remember, if a TV company wishes, you can be turned from saint to sinner at the flick of an editing switch.

Fame certainly has more negatives than plus points. But I would do it all over again and play *Big Brother* in exactly the same way.

And finally ...
A word on my 'co author' Mickey (coat-
tails) Hutton. He did absolutely nothing
in the creation of this book. I only
brought him along for the ride.